The ART of DOUBLES

Winning Tennis Strategies

The ART of DOUBLES

Winning Tennis Strategies

PAT BLASKOWER

BETTER
WAY
BOOKS

Cincinnati, Ohio

The Art of Doubles: Winning Tennis Strategies. Copyright © 1994 by Pat Blaskower. Illustrations © Douglas Redfern. Printed and bound in the United States of America. All rights reserved. No part of this book may be reproduced in any form or by any electronic or mechanical means including information storage and retrieval systems without permission in writing from the publisher, except by a reviewer, who may quote brief passages in a review. Published by Betterway Books, an imprint of F&W Publications, Inc., 4700 East Galbraith Road, Cincinnati, Ohio 45236. 1-800-289-0963. First edition.

06   05   04   11   10   9   8

Library of Congress Cataloging-in-Publication Data

Blaskower, Pat
    The art of doubles : winning tennis strategies / by Pat
  Blaskower.—1st. ed.
        p.   cm.
    Includes index.
    ISBN 1-55870-330-6
    1. Tennis—Doubles. I. Title
GV1002.8.B57   1993
796.342'28—dc20   93-31933
                                          CIP

Edited by Diana Martin
Designed by Brian Roeth

About the Author

 Pat Blaskower began playing tennis at the age of three, becoming a local junior champion at age twelve. In her career as a senior player, she has focused on the game of doubles. She has been ranked number one in the nation in Women's 35 Doubles; number one in northern California in Women's Open Doubles, Women's 35 Doubles and Women's 40 Doubles; and number two in northern California in Women's 45 Doubles. She coaches league teams in Marin County and is the head tennis professional at the Mill Valley Tennis Club.

Pat has a degree in English literature from the University of California in Berkeley.

Born in Jacksonville, Florida, Pat has lived in Marin County, California, for most of her adult life.

Author's Note

Personal pronouns are an anathema to the writer trying to talk to both genders. Somehow I just couldn't deface my text with a million "he/she's" or "him/her's." Therefore, since my first book was truly written for women, it is the male personal pronoun's turn. If you are a "she" reading this, please accept my apologies and know that it is all meant just as much for you, for her, as it is for him, since "it" was not a logical choice.

Acknowledgments

I owe a debt of gratitude to my shelty, Molly, who took a leave of absence from her job of chasing flies in the backyard to lie by my desk for countless hours. Also, I would like to thank: Sally Porter for transforming millions of sheets of yellow tablet covered with scribbles into a miracle that can be sent to a publisher over telephone lines; Doug Redfern for his exquisite artistry in the illustrations and for his wonderful sense of humor in the cartoons; Helen Harper for her patience and support; my doubles partner, Susan McShannock, who kept hounding me to "just write a book"; and, finally, Karla Clark, without whom pen would never have touched paper.

TABLE OF CONTENTS

FOREWORD

There is no better teacher than a student's thoughtfully posed question. Since the enormous success of *Women's Winning Doubles*, I have thought much, learned much from my students, and written too little. Yet this book has virtually been playing tag in my head almost from the day *Women's Winning Doubles* was published.

Women's Winning Doubles was written for a group of women whom I felt were either neglected or not accorded proper respect for their goals and expectations on the tennis court. This book is the sum of my experience to date, both as a doubles player and a teacher of the game. It is written for any serious student of the grace and intricately beautiful movement of a great doubles team.

INTRODUCTION

Why do some doubles teams look like wooden soldiers and others like a pair of dancers whose movements are synchronized and choreographed to the sound of music only they can hear? All that running around on the court—where are they going? How do they know where to be?

There are, essentially, three kinds of doubles teams: those who make things happen, those who watch what happens, and those who wonder what the hell happened.

Did you ever play against a doubles team that didn't seem to be particularly flashy, whose stroke production seemed inferior to yours, who didn't serve any aces or make many winners, and yet when it was all over, hadn't allowed you to win very many points, particularly the last one? Doubles isn't about big forehands and aces and crowd-stunning winners. It is a subtle game of grace, ball placement and movement whose masters often make others feel foolish or simply tempt them to beat themselves.

Players who watch what happens come in many varieties. There's the "I don't need court position because I can make a hole in your navel" species. Then there's the "Come to the net all you want, sucker, because I'll just lob you and watch you chase it" tribe. And finally, there's the Golden Retriever type, who, with patience to match the sunny disposition the breed is noted for, will just get every ball back into play. They wait, contentedly, for you to finally lose patience and control and hit the fence with your easy putaway, and they watch, panting and smiling with victory, as you explode your $200 graphite racket into the net post.

Players who wonder what the hell happened also come in several varieties, none of which is famous for tactical or strategic prowess. Some are devout baseliners, committed to the theory that doubles is just like singles without as much court to cover. Others distrust the mystery of doubles and tend to disparage those things that they do not understand and are not curious or courageous enough to learn. These are the players whom you have heard say, "I can't think and play at the same time. I just hit the ball." Freely translated, this means, "You can fill your head with fancy strategy all you want, but if I hit the ball hard enough at you, you'll probably miss, so why do I need all those expensive strategy lessons?" These players seldom recognize or acknowledge superior skills across the net, generally chalking up their losses to the windy conditions on their side of the net, the shadows across the court, poor lighting, tamale pie for lunch, a new, too old or not broken-in racquet, or the always useful pulled muscle.

The what-the-hell-happened players provide the naiveté of the doubles world, and it is to these species that I attribute what are probably the ten most misguided statements about doubles play, which will be exposed as the endeavors of fools.

1. The player whose forehand is in the center always takes the center ball.
2. When my partner is serving, he takes the lob over my head and I cross, but remain at the net.
3. I never poach at the net because I'll get in my partner's way. Better to let him take the ball.
4. I never come to the net on my second serve.
5. There is no point to "serve and volley tennis" because you just get lobbed all the time.
6. I like to play the deuce court because my forehand is so good (right-handed misguided statement).
7. When my partner is pulled wide, I must follow him, maintaining our No More Than Ten Feet Apart Axiom.
8. I like to hit deep service returns.
9. The best way to win a point at the net is to hit right at an opponent.
10. If our team is getting lobbed, I just stay back and leave my partner at the net.

Neither category of doubles team, not those who watch what happens nor those who wonder what the hell happened, possesses sufficient weapons to bother the highly skilled team, whose superior court position and shot selection combine to dispatch the pretenders-to-the-doubles-throne rather quickly. However, young and inexperienced teams are often very frustrated in their attempts to beat players whose skill levels, court position and tactics they recognize as inferior to their own. This disparity between the longed-for success in the future and the short-term bitter setback is a prime reason rising young teams become disillusioned and ultimately abandon the quest. As a coach, I send uninitiated and eager teams out to play matches every day, only to have them return with their tails between their legs because they were crucified by the dreaded "lob queens." It is vital for players who aspire to be great doubles specialists to understand that it takes time to build the expertise and teamwork necessary for success. It takes far longer to develop a great volley, a penetrating overhead, good anticipation, and a feel for your partner's court position and shot selection than it does to learn to hit a decent lob and a good drive from the base line. If you and your partner commit the time necessary to become an accomplished team, you will discover that by making things happen you can continue to improve as long as you play the game and that the "watchers" and "wonderers" are forever stuck with a deck of cards that has no aces.

There are elements in common to all teams that truly make things happen to their advantage on the tennis court. Time and again it becomes apparent that all great doubles teams appear to do the same things in very similar ways. It is not easy to quantify artistry, but that particular combination of elements inherent in the performances of distinguished doubles teams has the power to dispatch both the "watchers" and "wonderers" without missing a step and create marvelous theater for the spectator.

Often these players do not possess superior stroke production. A one-hundred-mile-per-hour serve is not a strict requirement for an effective doubles player. The ability to bounce an overhead over the back fence is not essential. Further, this book is not about technical skills. It is about court position and graceful movement and the intelligent understanding of those intangible factors that may not be obvious from the sidelines, but which combine to keep a great doubles team's winning percentage consistently high. It is about these ten elements in common displayed by all successful doubles partnerships:

1. Emotional and technical balance
2. Communication
3. Proper court position
4. Intelligent shot selection
5. Superior poaching skills
6. Keeping control of the net
7. Understanding the different jobs on the court
8. Flexibility
9. Mental toughness
10. Command of the intangibles

CHAPTER ONE

Creating and Nurturing a Balanced Doubles Team

Imagination reveals itself in the balance or reconciliation of opposite or discordant qualities: of sameness, with difference.
Samuel Taylor Coleridge

Picking the right person to share your tennis life with is no small matter. If you have aspirations to win national doubles titles, whether it be in the U.S. Open or as a 45-year-old senior champion, it is very serious business indeed. Even if your goals extend no further than local league play, the decision should be weighed more carefully than, "Hey, you wanna play?"

THE DREAM TEAM

Your own version of "the dream team" should take into consideration not only your strengths and weaknesses as a player, but also your ability to complement a potential partner's expertise.

When Billy Talbert and Bruce Old wrote *The Game of Doubles in Tennis* (published in 1956, it is regarded by many as the best book on doubles strategy ever written), they chose George M. Lott, Jr., John E. Bromwich, Donald Budge, and Jack Kramer as the best doubles players in the world and proceeded to ask each of them what they would look for in a perfect tennis partner. Their answers are as relevant to the game today as they were nearly forty years ago:

To choose the perfect, or dream doubles player, there are, of course, many things to look for. However, after giving it much thought, these are the requirements that I would prefer. It goes without saying that this player must possess all of the basic shots, and perhaps excel in a few. He would forget all about trying to serve aces except for rare occasions, and concentrate on getting his first serve in as consistently as possible. He would at all times play his volleys deep and down the middle, using the alleys only when they were wide open, but even then hating himself whilst doing so. (However, the time deep volleys wouldn't be logical would be if the four players were in at the net; then a short or low shot at the opponent's feet is the answer . . .) He should be able to play defensively as well as offensively. And he should have the type of personality that encourages talk during a match: there is nothing worse to me than having a doubles partner that won't "talk it up." There are always times when things aren't going well in almost any match, and if you can talk about these with your partner in an honest way, you can usually circumvent them.

J. Donald Budge

As a first court doubles player (Mr. Bromwich is referring to the deuce court), I feel that to achieve success it is most essential for the player to understand the value of service returns which he must make with regular consistency. Returning-of-service is so important, and ability to appreciate the strength of your opponents against varying returns is essential. The player in *the first court should endeavor to win the first point of each service, enabling his partner to try to force home the advantage and thus effect a breakthrough. He should be content to work for openings, be consistent with this return and prepared to forsake spectacular play in the best interests of developing teamwork and understanding with his partner.*

John E. Bromwich

In commenting on the qualifications for the ideal doubles player, I would like to emphasize a factor which is all too often overlooked. . . . I want to stress anticipation. . . . The thing that separates the great from the near-great doubles players is the uncanny ability to anticipate the actions of their opponents. There are four parts to anticipation . . . placing your own shot and knowing what to look for . . . learning the give-away motions of stroke production . . . concentrating on the motions of the opponent as he is in the act of striking the ball . . . you and your partner shifting positions to meet the by-now well-anticipated return. Yes sir, give me a partner with the "feel" of anticipation and he will have made a long stride toward being the dream doubles player.

John A. Kramer

As we know, doubles is mainly a matter of getting a service break, and then hanging on for dear life. Therefore, it behooves us to devise ways and means to obtain that service break. One way, of course, is through sheer power, but so few of us are able to do that that it is necessary to rely on cunning and cleverness. I suggest that, like a baseball pitcher who throws his fast ball, curve, and change-of-pace ball all with the same motion, the doubles player learn to make a forehand drive, a lob, and a soft, tantalizing shot . . . with the same motion.

George M. Lott, Jr.

Not one of these experts is seeking the spotlight-grabbing power hitter who likes to hit through his opponents' navels. Each stresses intelligence, patience, communication, teamwork and artistic shot selection—skills that anyone with a commitment to becoming a winner can acquire.

Winners Hate Losing; Losers Hate Winning

A winner makes commitments. A loser makes promises. A winner says, "I'm good, but not as good as I want to be." A loser says, "I'm not as bad as a lot of other people." A winner listens. A loser just waits until it's his turn to talk.

Anonymous

If it were really true that it's not whether you win or lose that matters, but only how kindly you play the game, then the rules of tennis would not have included keeping score. The game is, after all, a competition designed to produce a victor. When shopping for a partner, bear in mind that winners hate losing and losers can't stand winning. Losers will find a way to fail in every close match you play, filling the air with excuses for every missed shot along the way. We all choke points and make mistakes, but a real loser has an emotional investment in continued failure and is frightened of being successful. Loss after loss becomes a very comfortable easy chair and the possibility of a win is an intolerable disturbance to the status quo. These are the players who say to their partners, "I'm so bad. I just can't hit a ball," or "Those guys across the net are just too good. Maybe we'll get a few points if they double fault." This kind of attitude is just too discouraging for a partner, and not likely to change without some serious soul-searching. Better to make sure you pick a winner—preferably a tall, fast and crafty winner.

Scenario for a Winner

Once you've canvassed the field and have your eye on a few winners, look for someone in this group who complements you emotionally. If you tend to rush through matches, sometimes even holding your breath during points, don't pick someone who is in as mad a rush as you are. Your play will look like the fast forward image on your VCR. You will never gain balance as a team and will probably wear each other out before the first set is over. Choose someone whose internal clock runs a little more slowly than yours and who can get you to pause and take an occasional deep breath. Conversely, if you are a plodder who prefers to think slowly and carefully, pick someone who can rev your motor a little and help you turn up the tempo of a match.

Emotional balance may not seem so vital, but it is critical to the rhythm of your teamwork. During a match, the time you spend not hitting a ball—the "between points" time—far exceeds the time you actually spend playing a point. What a team does during the "between points" time will often determine whether it can maintain momentum within a match, and whether it can steal momentum from the opposition while they are napping. In addition, the team that manages this "down" time better, using it to change strategy, suggest a play or give added encouragement to one another, will almost always be the victor in a tight match. If you and your partner have just lost a "must" service game, you have also lost momentum. A doubles team of two "fast forward" types is not likely to slow down in the next game and is probably not capable of the careful execution needed to wrest momentum back. These are the players who will try to "hurry up to catch up" and will likely make far too many unforced errors. The match may slip through their hands while they are bustling around the court. On the other hand, two plodders are likely to brood and sulk over the lost service game, thereby elating the opposition by their sullen behavior to the

point that momentum is so entirely in the opponents' hands that the match cannot be saved.

WHO PLAYS WHICH COURT?

Having chosen a tall, fast and smart winner who complements your emotional make-up, you must decide who should play which side of the court.

Most good doubles players serve down the middle at least 80 percent of the time. If both you and your partner are right-handed, consider putting the stronger backhand service return, and/or backhand volley, in the deuce (right) court and the stronger forehand service return and/or forehand volley, in the ad (left) court. If your partner is a lefty, contemplate his effectiveness in the ad court. Most lefties have an uncanny ability to step around a serve and execute a topspin forehand that drops on an onrushing server's shoes at a viciously sharp, short angle. Lefties seem to do this naturally in a way most right-handers can never hope to duplicate. If your partner is a left-hander, you might want him in the ad court simply for this wicked service return.

On a right-handed team, the player in the ad court will take most of the overheads. Make sure that player is up to the task. If you have a lefty in the ad court for that devastating service return, the lob down the middle is a problem and requires some fancy footwork adjustments by both players in order to assure that the ball can be played as an overhead. If your lefty partner is in the deuce court and you, a right-hander, are in the ad court, it could be a racquet-clashing free-for-all on the lob unless your communication is superb.

Finally, every team should have a "setter" and a "hitter." Often, though this is not a hard-and-fast rule, the "setter," as alluded to by John Bromwich in comments about the "first court player" in his discussion of his "dream doubles partner," plays the deuce court and should be both psychologically and technically suited to the role. This player should be content to set the point up and allow the ad court player to claim the glory. Steadiness and dependability, percentage tennis (see page 35 for a discussion of percentage tennis) and much "plain vanilla" should be this person's forte. The setter's skills should also allow extensive use of the offensive lob as a service return (since the ball carries over a right-hander's opponent's backhand and often produces a weak lob that can be handled as an overhead smash by a right-handed hitter positioned in the ad court).

The "hitter" should be the team member whose personality is more that of a risk-taker and whose technical skills include the ability to hit clean winners and low percentage returns of serve. This player is generally positioned in the ad court because the score is always uneven when he is returning serve. The ad court player receives serve at every "break point" (except the 15-40 point) and at the beginning of every service rotation in

a tiebreak. At certain critical points in the match, he must have the courage to go for the winner rather than rely on his opponent to make an error.

Not all of the factors leading to court assignments will fall on the proper side of the issue. You may own a rapier backhand but be a "setter" at heart. You may have a great overhead, but don't trust your right-handed forehand down the middle under pressure. Your partner may definitely be the "hitter," but is also wedded to the deuce court. Ultimately, you evaluate each of your strengths and arrange to display those while hiding your weaknesses as best you can. But regardless of the considerations, you both must return serve well. If you can't break serve, you can't beat anybody.

Nurture Team Character

Out of the balancing of sameness with difference comes the character of your team. Playing well *as a team* is the common goal, and each of you, while bringing unique contributions to the endeavor, is responsible for making sure that the confluence of skills results in a smoothly running machine. If your partner's lob volley is the envy of the circuit but you can't execute it, stop trying and keep enough balls in play to allow him to showcase it. If he gets anxious and worried when you're behind, develop the skills to keep his head in the match and learn to act confident and unconcerned. If he tends to become serious and withdrawn under pressure, balance it out.

Take a class in stand-up comedy. Trust your partner and his judgment. Have pride in your team and learn to carry yourselves confidently on the court—shoulders back, racquets up. You win together and you lose together.

THE DUMP

One of the most painful experiences in the life of a doubles player is the moment of the "dump." Whether you are the "dump-or" or the "dump-ee," it is not a pleasant experience and can seldom be managed without someone feeling rejected or ill-used.

There are times and situations in a partnership when it is in both players' best interests to find new partners and the split ends up mutually beneficial. And there are times when the "dump-or" perceives a real or imagined advantage to the breaking of the partnership while the "dump-ee" would have been quite content with the status quo.

Sometimes it takes playing together for as long as a year before partners discover that they are simply incompatible and don't complement one another's talents. It may be as obvious as two personalities that don't mesh or as subtle as an inability to regulate the internal clock speed. If you play your matches at a speed of around eight and your partner likes to perform down around four, it may be that rather than balancing one another, you make him rush his shots and he makes you yawn. If so, your team cannot establish a comfortable playing rhythm.

Two players learn to play doubles together at a certain stage of their development. They take lessons together, practice together and play tournaments together. Often one has the raw talent to blossom very quickly into a much more highly skilled player, and does, and the other has less natural ability and learns far more slowly and so becomes "the weaker player." Sometimes the player lagging behind perceives the situation and sometimes he doesn't, but the rising star always is aware of the difference. This is the most difficult problem a doubles partnership will ever have to face. Often the advanced player hangs with the situation, says nothing and ignores the problem, but the losses become frustrating and resentment can creep onto the court. Painful as it may be, the two players should frankly discuss and recognize the legitimate need for the budding star to move on.

Sometimes people's priorities change. A player may have been totally committed to the task of becoming a great doubles team only to find that he cannot spare his partner the practice time the team needs. Perhaps he finds that it is not activities unrelated to tennis that intrude, but rather his commitment to the game of singles. Singles matches are almost always played before doubles matches, and a player who finds himself consistently involved in long, three-set singles duels will simply not have the energy to finish a grueling doubles match. In this case the partnership should be amicably dissolved and the doubles specialist should seek someone whose priorities are not so fragmented.

In some cases, the partnership may be functioning on the court as well as can be expected for the level of experience the team has gained, but one of the players will become impatient and dissatisfied with the win-loss record. This kind of player tends to be a great critic of his partner's weaknesses and a poor analyst of his own abilities. He fails to understand that a winning record must be amassed slowly, through time and trial and error, and is unaware that victory cannot be purchased. This player seems to have a new partner every week, constantly blaming each discard for every match lost. He seeks the proverbial Rosetta stone, convinced that success lies just around the corner if only he had the perfect partner. A player dumped by this kind of partner is well rid of him and should rejoice.

Whether it be a legitimate difference over practice methods or doubles philosophy, incompatible personalities, or an aversion to gum-chewing, the decision to end the doubles relationship should be mutual.

When you commit your time and energy to learning the game of doubles with a partner, first and foremost, you have to really like that person. Second, you must trust that person. Third, you must respect that person. You will be in for as many rough days as splendid ones, as many failures as triumphs, as many disappointments as wonderful surprises, and how you treat each other under pressure will ultimately determine the health of your doubles partnership.

Balance Checklist

- ✔ Make sure you pick the right partner—one who complements you emotionally and technically.

- ✔ Consider carefully who should play the deuce court and who should play the ad court.

- ✔ Understand that teamwork means balance and that the goal is not to showcase one player, but rather to play well as a team.

- ✔ If your partnership just isn't working, dissolve it amicably.

- ✔ Treat your partner with respect, and the team will develop self-esteem.

CHAPTER TWO

Keep Your Team's Communication Lines Open

A fool may talk, but a wise man speaks.

Ben Johnson

Y ou are serving at 4-5 in the third set of a vital tennis match. A win means your entire USTA league team goes to a sectional competition. The score is 15-30. Your partner turns to you and says, "Come on. Get this point. We need it!" That statement pushes your heart rate and blood pressure close to those of someone critically ill. Your anxiety level goes off the chart and you're fortunate if your serve makes it to the net on three bounces. Your partner has made a common mistake. Rather than speak calmly and quietly about a plan for the point, the player succumbs to the pressure, abdicates all responsibility for this critical situation and really says to the server, *"You* do it! Please, God, don't let the ball come to me!" This kind of communication is so destructive that it may lose the match.

COMMUNICATION BEGINS OFF-COURT

Good communication between partners starts before you take the court and should include a brief discussion of the day's game plan, including strengths and weaknesses of opponents, if known. If your partner for the day isn't your regular partner, decide beforehand who will play which side of the court, who will serve first, and whether you will choose to serve or receive. Don't walk on the court and allow your opponents to witness a conversation such as this one:

"What side do you play?"

"Oh, I don't care. Do you?"

"No, not really. Shall I play forehand?"

"Ok. Shall we serve? We won the spin."

"Oh, I'm not real confident of my serve. You want to serve?"

After a discussion like this one, be assured that your opponents are, at best, supremely confident and, at worst, sure that you two are a couple of lunatics who quite possibly have no idea what you're doing.

All good doubles teams communicate frequently between points (sometimes after every point if it is a very critical game). They share ideas; give positive and specific suggestions for point-playing; encourage one another to stay confident; and even sometimes confess to anxiety or "choking." This kind of dialogue is much easier when you are winning and much harder, although more crucial, when struggling to reverse a losing situation.

Dr. Allen Fox, sports psychologist and contributing editor to *Tennis Magazine*, commenting on the psychology of tennis, said, "Winning requires solutions, not descriptions of problems." The player who spends valuable between-point time lamenting to his partner, "This sucks. I can't return serve. They're too good," is certainly describing the problem, but he appears to be fresh out of solutions. How much more constructive if that player would say instead, "I'm having trouble with that big serve. I'm going to try a lob. Be alert."

If we rejoin that anxious server at 4-5, 15-30, whose partner has just unwittingly rendered him nearly catatonic, how much more useful it would have been to say, "You serve down the middle and I'll poach the return." Any time a partner gives a suggestion for a particular serve or return or combination of shots, it alleviates some of the pressure and allows both players to share equally in the responsibility for the outcome of the point. Good doubles teams know this and experiment with solutions to problems. When things get rough, they never retreat into sulky silence leaving their partners alone, exposed to the enemy and fearful to utter even simple words of encouragement.

Golden Rules of Good Communication

• **In general, always err on the side of speaking too much, not too little.** Great doubles teams don't make assumptions and they don't leave things to chance. "Yours" or "Mine" should be uttered every time there is any question as to who will hit the shot. Thinking your partner is going to hit the ball, only to see it bounce unplayed on your side of the court is an example of assuming what should be carefully designated. Never stand idly by and watch your partner struggle to keep his eye on the ball and worry whether or not his feet are in the court and whether or not he might play an "out" ball. Always help with a clear and loud "Bounce it," if appropriate, or "Out!" if you believe it is going out. Never assume your partner can read your mind. If you intend to try a very wide serve on the next point, or a passing shot down the line, or if the score permits a low-percentage return, tell your partner your plan so that he can be ready before the opponent's play and not be surprised by it at the last minute.

• **Be aware of your body language.** Body language is probably the subtlest and most overlooked form of communication with your partner. Dr. Jim Loehr, author of *The Mental Game* and consultant to the USTA Junior Development Program, encourages players to "look on the outside the way you want your partner to feel on the inside." Nobody loses points on purpose, and if, when your partner blows the perfect set-up into the bottom of the net, you are a shoulder-slumper or a sigher or a hands-on-hips starer, it won't be long before your partner decides that the rules have been changed to permit three against one.

• **Trust your partner and never undermine him.** If you believe he blew a call, don't indicate to your opponents that you're either playing with a cheater or a candidate for bifocals. Tell your partner quietly that you believe the call to be in error and let *him* correct the mistake, thus preserving the team unity in your opponents' eyes. If you're about to hit a ball and your partner tells you to let it go, do it. Don't hit the ball anyway and then tell your partner that you know better which balls are good and which will sail out.

Trust on the court is a vital component of confidence.

• **Communication on the court must be a dialogue, not a state of the union address.** Many times one player will have no trouble being vocal while the other, perhaps shier, partner is content to listen and say very little. Players must share the responsibility equally for keeping the communication lines open since certain situations demand assertiveness from even the most timid teammate. For instance, in the role of server's partner, you will be a great help to your server if you have the courage to tell him where you would like him to serve, suggest a kind of spin, call different team formations, or even predict that a lob is in the offing. Shrinking violets have trouble assuming this responsibility, and yet doing so allows the serving partner the luxury of sharing the burden for winning the service game.

• **Both partners should communicate kindly, thoughtfully, positively and confidently even under the most adverse circumstances.** Each player must trust that his partner will be receptive to constructive criticism or suggestions for improving the team's performance, even though the chances for victory at a particular moment may be dismal. It is all too easy when things are going badly to become silent, withdrawn and essentially resigned to the inevitable loss. At this point in a match, many players actually become afraid to say anything to their partners. The courage to "talk it up," as Don

Budge puts it, must come from someone, so if it isn't forthcoming from your partner, then it must come from you.

• **Good communication built on trust also serves to avoid the ethical problems that sometimes arise.** Many players state, unequivocally, that they will never overrule a partner's call. Regardless of whether this refusal is out of fear of reprisal from the partner, or simply loyalty, it is nothing less than cheating. This scenario is one familiar to all players:

You serve what you think is an ace. Both you and your partner think the serve was good, so one of you asks the opponent who called the ball out if he is sure. "Yes," he says. Then you turn to his partner and politely ask if he saw the ball. "No, I didn't see it at all," he says. Maybe he really didn't see the ball, but if that team is a never-overrule-your-partner team, you can rest assured that he will *never* have seen *any* ball his partner calls out.

Call questionable balls their way, not yours; you lose the point but have your concentration, the grail of self-respect. Wear white. Mind losing.

from "Tennis"
by Howard Wilcox

Your tennis reputation is a vital part of your on-court presence, and unpleasant as it may be, you must overrule your partner's call if you clearly see a ball differently. Start with the assumption that you are both honest players and that each of you trusts the other's judgment. Given that information, it is reasonable to assume that everybody blows a call now and then. If your partner feels that you called a ball incorrectly, he should immediately tell you, softly, and you should make the correction to the opponents. The whole issue of line calls in tennis is such a charged one that players tend to overreact. If your team corrects a call that you have made in error, do not worry that your opponents will immediately brand you as cheaters. In fact, it is quite the opposite. By having the courage to reverse your own call, you will most certainly gain their respect.

• **Always present a united front.** Take the court together, sit together on the changeover, and leave the bench together after each rest period. Not only is this behavior important because it facilitates last-minute communication of ideas, but it also is designed to send important messages to your opponents.

Some opponents, whether deliberately or unwittingly, try to use the "divide and conquer" approach. Everyone knows that the time for polite chit-chat is *after* the match, never before or during, and yet some opponents will try to isolate one of you and solicit your attention, breaking your concentration and your unity as a team. If you remain together, this tends not to happen, as they are loathe to try to engage both of you. The minute one of you is sitting alone, you are subject to being taken under the wing of the enemy, thus leaving your poor partner the lone adversary.

My partner of several years ago (with whom I won a national doubles title) was a wonderfully tough competitor and also a kind, friendly and warmhearted individual. On one occasion we were playing a match in which we had quite a comfortable lead midway through the second set. At some point we lost a ball over a fence, which I offered to retrieve. When I returned to the court several minutes later, I found my partner and both of our opponents sitting on the bench together avidly discussing their mutual preferences in tennis clothes, shoes and racquets. When the match resumed, we quickly lost six straight games before we righted the ship, regained our concentration and closed out the match.

While you can control interaction with your opponents during a match, sometimes avoiding pre-match fraternization with the enemy is awkward. If you play league matches, you know that socializing is as much a part of the event as the competition, and it is very tough to maintain that balance between "putting on your game face" and being a gracious hostess to, or guest of, the other team. You and your partner must remember that the point of taking the court in the first place is to compete fairly but unmercifully, taking advantage of every miscue your opponents make. It becomes most difficult to maintain that attitude if you have just made,

minutes before the match, two new lifelong friends out of your opponents. The strategy that seems to work best for my students in this predicament is to use platitudes. Be polite and gracious, but do not get into a long conversation with your opponent-to-be about how your strained shoulder is feeling or how powerful his new racquet has proven to be. Save substantive conversations for *after* the match.

In the environs of a sanctioned tournament, it is often easier to avoid prematch interaction with your opponents because socializing is really the last thing on anyone's mind. Everyone has come to the event with the sole purpose of demolishing the opposition. Occasionally, however, unavoidable pitfalls arise.

In July of 1992, my partner and I played the Women's National Senior Grasscourt Championships in Haverford, Pennsylvania. The event is played, for as long as the weather holds, on the most beautiful grass courts in the world. That year a torrential thunderstorm descended upon us on the day of the semifinals, drenching the courts and, in the groundskeeper's words, "closing the grass" for the remainder of the tournament. Matches were completed not on *twenty-five* grass courts, but rather on *four* carpeted indoor courts. Obviously, scheduling became chaotic, and as many as one hundred players were crowded into a small viewing area awaiting their turn to play.

Avoiding our opponents became nearly

15

impossible unless we chose to stroll through the deluge outside. One of the women we were scheduled to play cornered my partner and explained that these indoor courts were virtually her "home turf." She bragged of her ability to hit every line on the court, indicated that she and her partner were the "home crowd favorites" since they lived in the area, and questioned the expertise of two Californians not only on the now-soggy grass, but also on a carpet we had never set foot on. I was well aware of what was happening, but short of being rude to someone enjoying the support of the club members who were hosting this tournament, I could do nothing. I decided our psychological rebuttal would have to wait for the match.

When it was finally our turn to play, my partner took the court nervous and a little shaky. Our garrulous opponent was still at it, chattering away at my partner. I said nothing. In the first game of the match, on the first point our friend served to me, I hit a forehand service return between the two opponents for a winner. The next time she served to me, I was able to win the point with a volley I hit right at her navel (not generally my first choice of targets). At this point, I had silenced the biased crowd and muzzled our chatterer. My partner settled down and proceeded to play some of the best tennis of her career, earning applause and respect from the audience. We went on to win the match, but it was a struggle.

I believe we would have won the match in any case because we were the better team, but clearly the prematch interaction between our opponent and my partner (couched in the guise of polite conversation but obviously intended as psychological warfare) was an obstacle we would rather not have had to deal with.

Finally, in an unofficiated match, the most uncomfortable moment on the court comes when a team needs to call for a linesperson. This puts a tremendous strain not only on the lines of communication between the team members, but also on your ability to communicate further with your opponents. If you feel that your opponents are repeatedly making incorrect line calls, you simply must stop the match and ask the tournament officials for help. Often one team member will feel that the situation warrants a linesperson but is loathe to do so for fear of upsetting either his partner or the opposition or both. A conversation between partners might sound like this:

"That's the third time my ball has hit the back line and they've called it out." (Translation: "Those guys are cheating and I want to call for a linesperson.")

"Hey, partner, just ignore it and aim a little shorter." (Translation: "Don't you dare make waves. I don't want to be embarrassed and have people think we're bad sports. Our opponents would probably never speak to us again. They're very nice people and probably just need glasses.")

In order to avoid the embarrassment and

the divisiveness of this situation, teammates should discuss their strategy for this eventuality before they ever begin the match. Both players need to understand that they have a right to expect proper line calls from their opponents, and if fairness is not forthcoming, the outcome of the match may be jeopardized unless they take steps to correct the situation. Calling for a linesperson can be done quietly and gracefully, as simply as, "I think we need some help out here," and doing so does not label your team troublemakers or monsters. If it becomes necessary to ask for help, stand united as a team. Don't let one partner make the unpleasant declaration while the other runs to the net wringing his hands and apologizing profusely to the opponents for the inconvenience.

Any time you call a linesperson to your court, further necessary communication across the net becomes strained at best. A team must understand that this is an unfortunate but unavoidable consequence of their actions and resign themselves to suffer it stoically. A tennis match is not a popularity contest and the goal is not to endear yourselves to your opponents but rather to emerge victorious — fairly and honestly. If, having requested the assistance of an impartial observer, you question the wisdom of your decision, evaluate the end result. If the questionable calls stopped after the arrival of the linesperson, then you halted deliberate cheating. If the same calls were made, only to be overruled by the linesperson, then your opponents were probably fair people in desperate need of an optometrist.

In all facets of life, the ability to communicate well is a learned skill, and it is always more difficult in a crisis. As with all dimensions of your tennis game and your teamwork, communication must be practiced to be effective. The results are well worth the effort.

Communication Checklist

- ✔ Communicate well with your partner, as this strategy often makes the difference between a win and a loss in a tight match.

- ✔ Battle the tendency to "shut down" emotionally when things are tight. Talk more, not less, under pressure.

- ✔ Never take the enemy under your wing, or vice versa.

- ✔ Don't be timid. Stand up for your rights — together, as a team.

CHAPTER THREE

Learn Proper Court Position

Reason, in itself confounded,
Saw division grow together.

W. Shakespeare

Court position is one of the few things in this wonderfully maddening game that is entirely under your control as a player and as a team. You may not be able to handle an opponent's booming serve and you probably can't prevent him from mishitting winners off his frame, but you can certainly put yourself in the right position on the court to deal with whatever is hurled your way.

Many, many players are wedded to the notion that proper court position is wherever you happen to be at the moment. The "watcher" or "wonderer" of the doubles court is frequently on the base line, leaving his partner alone, unhappy and far too vulnerable at the net. This "one up, one back" formation will beat teams whose skills are technically inferior. However, if you put two doubles teams of equal technical skill on a court, with one team in proper position at the net and the other in a "one up, one back" formation, the net team will win the match nine out of ten times—possibly ten out of ten. Baseball teams have center fielders; tennis teams do not. Good doubles teams—those that have the ability to make things happen—will always make you pay for poor court position by exploiting the enormous holes left gaping by a "one up, one back" team. In addition to all of the other misery this formation invites (bickering between partners and

LEARN PROPER COURT POSITION

arguing about the center ball), leaving your partner exposed at the net is tantamount to asking him to wear a target inscribed, "Attention opponents: Hit the ball at me. I am defenseless." And they will happily oblige.

WHAT, EXACTLY, IS PROPER COURT POSITION?

"Court position" refers only to your team's distance from the net, not the distance between the two partners. Relative to that, there are only two places on the court for your team to be positioned; one offensive, one defensive. The offensive court position can be defined as "second volley position," or "the offensive line." (See diagram 1.) It is an area on the court about two steps *behind* the centers of both service boxes. Consider it "home base," from which you rove throughout a point. The defensive court position (see diagram 1) is situated approximately two feet *behind* the base line. The offensive position is the goal a team must attain after the point starts. The defensive position is one forced on a team by the opposition. Inexperienced teams are often shocked to learn that the best offensive position on the court is so far from the net, and the best defensive court position is so far outside the base line. There is no such animal as a "net-hugging" court position. You never start a point "on the net," but you may earn the right to close the net later in the development of the point.

Once you have attained second volley position within the point, keeping it takes work. To maintain your advantage, you and your partner must be able to handle balls that opponents try to hit through you, by you, between you and over you (chapter six has been devoted to balls people attempt to hit over you). While in your offensive court position, your team should be in constant lateral motion, continuously making appropriate court position adjustments.

THE WALL AXIOM

Whose ball is the center ball, anyway? More often than not balls hit up the middle in doubles have come from either the ad or deuce side of the court and thus have an angle as they cross the net. Who takes the center volley is one of the least understood and most argued about facets of doubles. This is the time when the "wonderer" steps in to take the ball because he has the forehand in the middle. I have always been amused by the presumption that his forehand volley is better than his partner's backhand volley.

Although your team may have attained second volley position, you should nevertheless remain in constant lateral motion in order to keep all passing shots from penetrating and landing untouched. I call this movement the "wall" action, and the formula concerning the center ball the Wall Axiom.

The Wall Axiom says, simply: The center ball is always yours on the diagonal and your lateral court position adjustment should re-

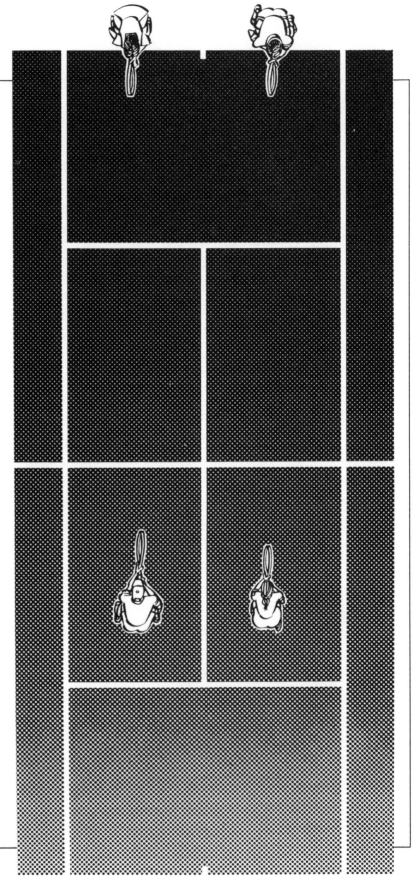

Diagram 1
Second Volley Plus Defensive Court Positions

The team in the foreground properly holds second volley position and is prepared to deal with either lobs or potential passing shots hurled at them from the opposing team, which is properly positioned in the defensive court position behind the base line.

flect that knowledge before the ball is hit. If the ball on the other side of the net is *not* on a diagonal from you, but rather is directly *opposite* you, mirror your opponent, remaining in the middle of the probable angles of return. (See diagram 2.)

While this axiom may sound very erudite and complicated, it is really quite simple, and there are *no exceptions*. Balls that are high, slow and without a severe angle should be poached (see chapter five for more information about poaching) and put away, but since you dare not change the angle of a low ball, or poach a low, hard-hit ball, whether it be off a service return or in the middle of a point, you and your partner need to know without taking the time to analyze the situation, who will play the center ball. For example, you only have one opponent at a time— the person about to strike the ball. If you are the deuce court player and you hit the ball toward your opponent's deuce court, you should move laterally so that you crowd the middle, *before* your opponent strikes the ball. Consequently, you will be perfectly positioned to play any ball hit toward the middle of your court. (See diagram 3.) You won't have to change the ball's angle or leave too much of your own court exposed while you chase down a ball angling away from you. Meanwhile, your partner becomes the "mirror" of the deuce court player, moving wide if his opponent does, or moving to the middle if his opponent does. If your team then hits the ball into your opponents' ad court, you

and your partner shift responsibilities. You become the mirror and he positions himself near the center service line, expecting to play the center ball.

If you are a right-handed player in the deuce court and you shift left to cover the middle, be aware that you might also have to play a *forehand* volley. Be alert to your opponent trying to hit a crosscourt passing shot by you. Conversely, the ad court player whose turn it is to cover the center should be on the lookout for a passing shot aimed crosscourt toward his *backhand* volley. *However, because of the geometry of the court, the farther away from the net your opponent is, the less likely this kind of a shot will be successful and the more likely the ball will sail wide and out.*

The Wall Axiom is percentage tennis, reflecting the way in which all good doubles teams move at the net. It applies whether your opponents are at the net or on the base line. This positioning will not protect you against opponents' clean winners or if you pop volleys up to opponents' racquets waiting six feet above the net.

The wall does not care whether you are left-handed, right-handed or ambidextrous. However, if you are still in love with "forehand takes the middle," here is good news: If your team plays the ball directly down the middle to your opponents' "T," it will be nearly impossible for its return to have an angle. This is the time for "forehand takes the middle" if you wish, *but* it is really better

Diagram 2
The Wall Axiom, Part 1

*The ad court player, toward whom
the ball is traveling, has shifted his
court position laterally toward the
middle of the court in advance of the
strike of the ball. It is not enough to
understand that the center ball is
yours and prepare to dive for it after
it is struck, because it will go past
your racquet before you can react.
Your court position should reflect the
knowledge that the center ball is
yours on the diagonal before the ball
is struck.*

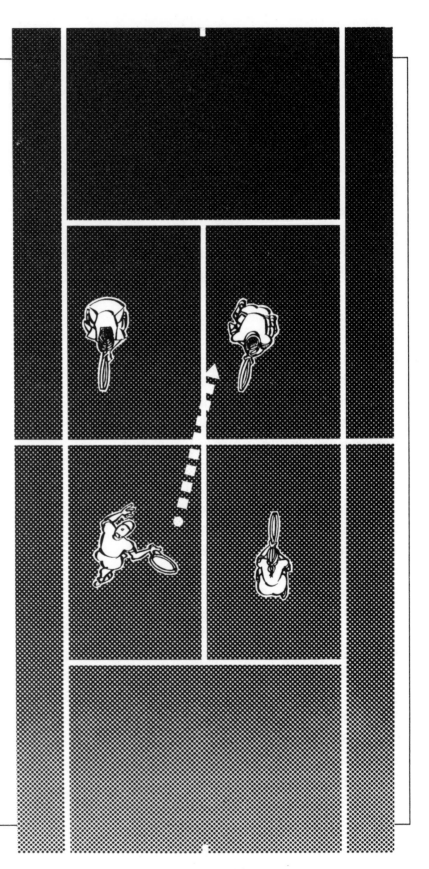

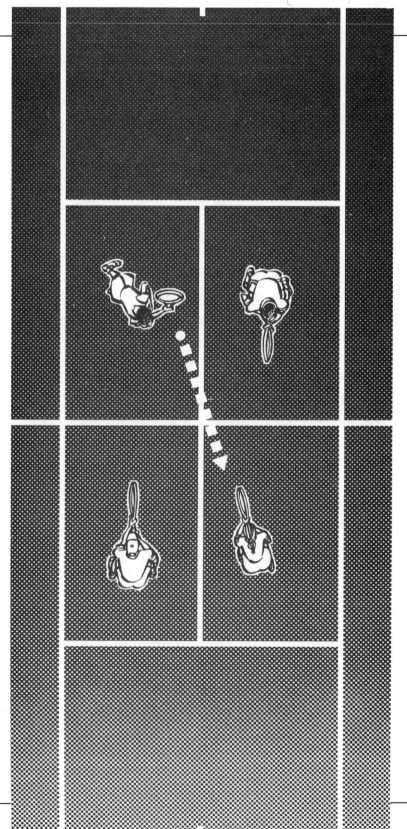

Diagram 3
The Wall Axiom, Part 2
Both deuce court players have shifted toward the center service line in order to insure that each can easily reach the ball aimed down the middle on the diagonal. At the same time, each must be alert to the possibility of a forehand volley. Both ad court players are "mirroring" their opponent since each of these players is, alternately, directly opposite the ball rather than on the diagonal from it.

to play "the guy who just hit the last ball hits the next," because he is the player with the momentum going toward the net.

Many players erroneously believe that they should never be more than about ten feet apart on the court, acting as if they are tied together by an invisible string. When one of the team is pulled wide (toward the alley) to play a ball, the partner quickly shuffles over to maintain that ten-foot distance between them, leaving about a twenty-eight foot wide area unprotected. This is a serious tactical error that provides your opponents with far too much open court. If you bear in mind that *all* court position adjustments are made as a result of where the ball lands on the *opposite* side of the net and not where it lands in your court, you will avoid making this mistake. (See diagram 4.)

Even if your partner has had to dive into his alley to retrieve a sharply angled volley and is, as a result, draped along the side fence exhausted, you can sit down and have coffee until the ball lands again in your opponents' court, and then, as always, the Wall Axiom applies.

If your partner, whom we shall assume is now lying prone in his alley, manages to play the ball down the line, he is, in effect, asking you for help because the ball is now on the diagonal *from you*. You should put your coffee cup in your pocket and move quickly to the center to fulfill your wall responsibilities.

Remember, the "center" of the court moves; you need to always anticipate where it will be. If an opponent who is diagonal from you aims a ball down the center of the court at you, and he is out of the court and wide of his alley when he strikes the ball, you should be positioned well into your partner's service box in order to properly intercept it. If your prone partner plays the ball crosscourt, so it is opposite you, execute the "mirror" portion of your wall duties while your partner picks himself up, scrambles back and covers the center ball. (See diagram 5.) No matter how dire your partner's emergency, do *not* run over there only to be near him. He needs you more when your opponents have the ball.

The Wall Axiom is not a perfect solution for all possible situations, but it should stop you from feeling like Swiss cheese or wondering how wide your partner is or how far you should reach for a ball. It should also help you understand what happens when a ball passes untouched between you and your partner and should give you the skills to rectify the problem quickly, instead of having to go through five minutes of:

"That was mine."

"No. That was mine."

"Maybe it was just too good."

"Naw. I should have had it."

This dialogue never really comes to a helpful conclusion. It's not a perfect world and it's not a perfect wall, but it's better than the above conversation.

Diagram 4
Assess Your Partner's Shot Before Moving
The ad court player in the foreground has been pulled wide to hit the volley, but his partner waits to see where the ball is played before adjusting his court position.

Diagram 5
Choices From a Wide Court Position

The ad court player who has been pulled wide has two options. He may play his volley down the line and thus require his partner to cover the center ball on the diagonal. Or he may play his volley crosscourt, making it clear that he can recover in time to cover the center ball and is thus asking his partner to mirror the opponent.

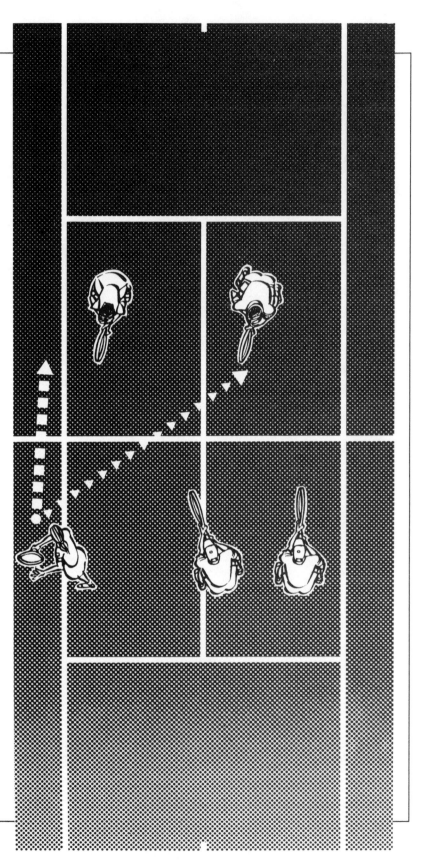

PLACES ON THE COURT

While there is no team court position closer to the net than the second volley position, adjustments to the ball may be necessary, and should be made *only* by the player expecting to strike the ball. Meanwhile, the partner always maintains second volley position while awaiting his teammate's return. If one partner drifts slightly behind the service line to hit an overhead, the other should stay put. If one takes a step or two forward to play a volley, the other does not mimic his partner's footwork. That is totally counterproductive.

However, there are times when a player must, to play a ball, make a court adjustment so extreme that he cannot be expected to have recovered his court position on the next ball. In these cases, his partner makes a "protective" court adjustment until such time as the team regains second volley position.

For example, an opponent's "floater"—a barely moving, soft, high ball—requires that one partner "close the net." This move, correctly executed, will put him so close to the net that he may be in danger of touching it. This is the most aggressive move in doubles. He becomes a terminator, and the ball should not come back, but *if it does*, he is totally out of position and *any* ball will be over his head. This is the time for the partner, observing the closing move, to adjust by drifting out of second volley position and claiming a position close to the "T" in order to be the "head protector" and cover the lob, in the

unlikely event that the ball comes back. (See diagram 6.) Both players should make every effort to regain second volley position as soon as is practical, taking care not to be in motion when an opponent is hitting a ball.

Playing a deep overhead is also a time when both players will have to make a court adjustment. If you see your partner fading three or four feet behind the service line to hit an overhead, it is unlikely that he can regain his offensive position by the time the opponent's ball crosses the net again. In this case, adjust slightly forward of second volley position in order to become "toe protector," hoping to be able to terminate a ball that would otherwise land at your partner's out-of-position feet. Readjust as your partner gains second volley position. (See diagram 7.)

Extreme court adjustments do not mean that a team has relinquished its offensive position. Ideally, the goal of the good doubles team is to get into the second volley position, hold it, and win the majority of the points from there. In reality, it is a rare match that is fought solely from that place. Adjustments to the ball predominate most points and a good team will appear to be in a staggered formation more often than not. The partner who has drifted well behind the service line to smash an overhead has no intention of making that spot a court *position*, nor does the player who has "closed" the net intend to remain two inches from the netstrap for the duration of the point. Winning points requires this movement out of "home base"

Diagram 6
Being a "Head Protector"
The ad court player in the foreground is closing the net in order to put the volley away and end the point. In the unlikely event that the ball comes back, his deuce court partner has drifted back to cover a potential lob, executing his duty as "head protector."

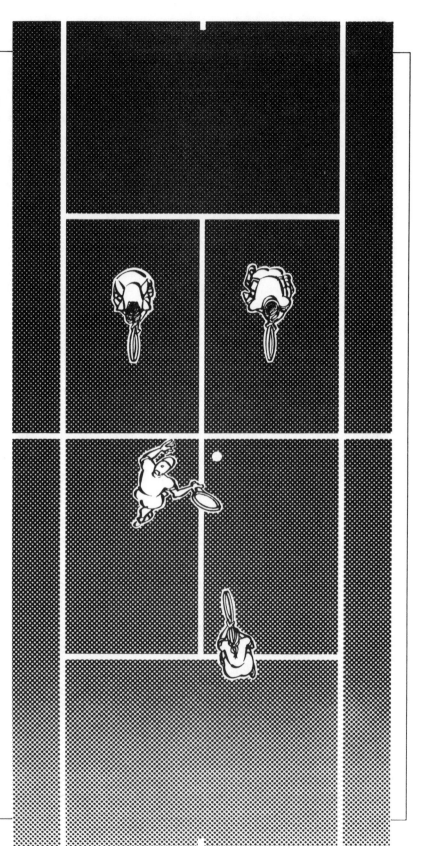

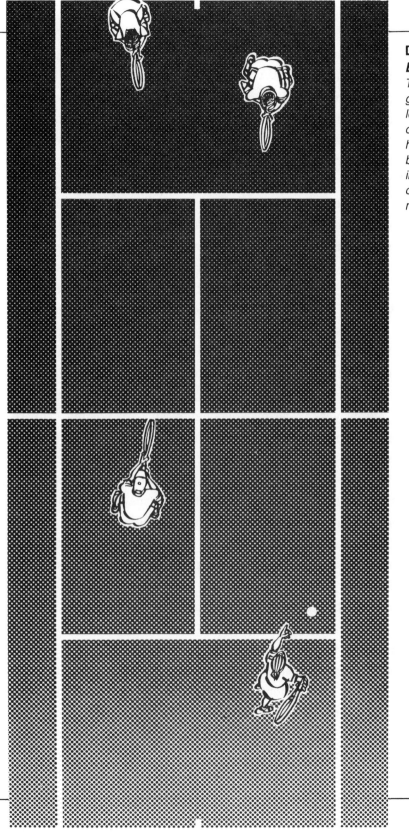

Diagram 7
Being a "Toe Protector"
The deuce court player in the foreground has drifted out of second volley position in order to smash an overhead. His partner in the ad court has momentarily closed the net to become "toe protector," looking to intercept a soft floater that would otherwise bounce in front of his partner's feet.

position if the ball is to be played properly. If it takes several overheads or more than one angled volley to end the point, the team may remain staggered until the conclusion of the point. In reality, when your team is on offense, proper court position becomes one partner protecting the other's vulnerability so that the net does not have to be relinquished. One player closes and the other drifts. If toes and heads are protected, offense is preserved.

Moving to Defensive Position

When a ball manages to sail over your team's heads and lands anywhere near the base line, you are deemed to have lost your offensive court position. In this situation one player should lob the ball back, but *both* players should retreat to their defensive court position—several feet behind the base line—and await the proper moment to reclaim the net together. Having arrived behind the base line, you cannot decide you simply don't want to be there and go charging wildly forward like a person terrified of ground strokes.

Regaining the net is a "time and distance" problem and both players must be patient. Assuming that your opponents now have control of the net, and assuming that one of them is about to hit an overhead smash off your lob, it is unlikely that you could play a ball landing deep in your court and then run fast enough to reclaim second volley position before your opponent strikes the ball again. (Remember: Do not be in

motion when your opponent is hitting a ball.)

When forced to play defense, be very careful of your court position. Do not be tempted to creep forward bit by bit, hoping your opponents won't notice. They will. And they will volley behind you. There is no situation on the court that demands more patience and discipline from a team than this one. Rather than eagerly anticipating the first opportunity to reclaim the net, experienced teams will "dig in" and resign themselves to the unpleasant fact that the point may well have to be won by playing good defense. In the course of playing one of these points, you may receive a short ball that you or your partner could play on the rise and as a result, regain the net, but then you must approach against opponents who are holding firm, remaining entrenched in their offense position. While it is not a tactical error to use a short ball as an approach shot to a net already held by the opposition, it may be an ill-advised and hasty decision. When you move forward and play a ball on the rise, you increase your chances of making an unforced error, such as putting the ball into the net. It is worth considering that a team playing good defense is very apt to bore an aggressive net team to death. There is no other situation more likely to produce a sloppy error from an impatient net team than that in which they face a series of irksome lobs and tiresome ground strokes. Rather than using that short ball as an approach shot, it is far less risky to hit just one more boring lob. Possibly that's the

DON'T TRY TO SNEAK BACK TO YOUR OFFENSIVE VOLLEY POSITION ON A TEAM ALREADY ENTRENCHED AT THE NET, THEY WILL VOLLEY BEHIND YOU. DIG IN AND PLAY DEFENSE.

one your opponent sprays into the back fence. And if it's not, it might be the next one.

Regaining the Net

There are only two ways to regain the net: 1) wait for a ball that bounces short enough on your side of the net to allow you to move near your offensive position, making the time and distance problem manageable; 2) relob your opponents well enough that they must chase the ball, which will give you the time to reach second volley position before your opponents can return the lob. If your team is fortunate enough to get a chance to reclaim the net, be sure that you move forward together and are set in second volley position for the next shot. (See diagram 8.)

Nowhere in this discussion of court position have I mentioned "first volley position," and that is because I have eliminated it from my vocabulary and my teaching. I believe that it does not matter where you are on the court when you play your first volley as long as you are moving forward when you play the ball. Players seem to make a better and more forcing shot if they move through the first volley, arriving balanced and ready to continue the point from second volley position. First and second volleys still exist, but I no longer believe that a "first volley *position*" is necessary.

If position in life is everything, then court

Diagram 8
Regaining Net Control

When forced to play defense, be patient. You can only reclaim the net by lobbing over your opponents and forcing them to retreat to retrieve the ball, or you must receive a ball that lands very close to your second volley position so that you can manage your time and distance problems.

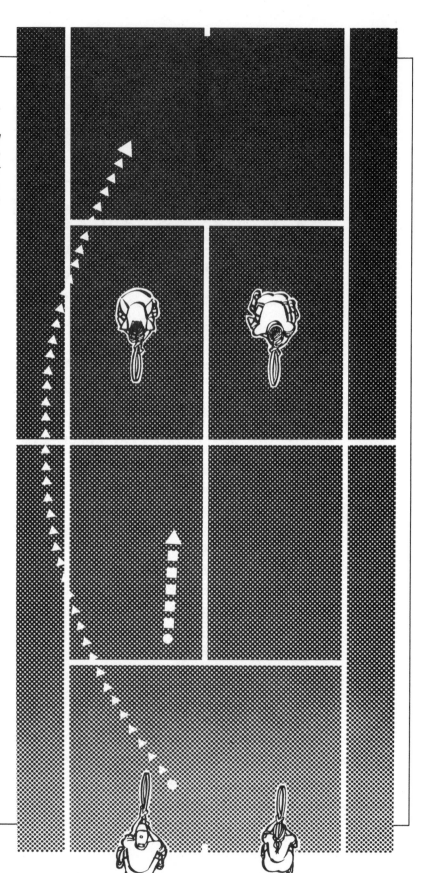

position in doubles is everything. Do not cheat it by developing even a slight case of "base line creep," for without proper court position you most assuredly will seldom win. Do not neglect it by blaming a weak second serve for your wish not to take the net, because superior court position will often let you steal a match from those with superior skills. Remember that court position is the one thing that is entirely under your control. If you control your environment you create options for your team, and intelligent shot selection is predicated on having numerous options.

Court Position Checklist

✔ Remember that court position in doubles is more important than stroke production.

✔ The center ball belongs to the player on the diagonal from the ball.

✔ Expect to stagger your team formation in order to maintain the offensive court position.

✔ Defend the court from behind the base line by relying on all your patience and discipline.

CHAPTER FOUR

Win With Intelligent Shot Selection

It is circumstance and proper timing that give an action its character and make it either good or bad.

Agesilaus

Most ill-advised shot selection is due to a player's desire to end a point much too early. Every tennis point has a beginning, a middle and an end, and while your opponent may do you the favor of making an error early on, most points that you successfully complete must be won in stages. Inexperienced aspiring teams, along with the "watchers" and "wonderers," fail to comprehend that the rules of tennis are written with the presumptions that the ball will be returned and that there are people out there who can and will handle your best shot. Great doubles teams recognize this state of affairs as unavoidable and actually look forward to the challenge of a long rally, whereas "hoping no one will get to the ball" seems to be the prime motivation for unintelligent shot selection.

The beginning of a point includes only the serve and service return. The middle of the point extends from the first volley through all subsequent shots played up to the one that will end the point. The end of the point is simply the one ball that does not come back into play. Players lacking in confidence or those who become overanxious tend to try to reverse this order and generally make a high number of unforced errors. Experienced doubles teams know they must be equally as intelligent in their choice of shots for the beginning of the point as they are for both the middle and the end of the point.

PERCENTAGE TENNIS

High-percentage shot selection or "straight vanilla," as I say to my students, can be defined as using the best and most appropriate speed, spin and direction on any ball, given your distance from the net, the height of the ball you must play, and your opponents' court positions. It includes careful consideration of the score and where the momentum of the match lies. It is always the shot that, under the circumstances, has the highest probability of clearing the net and landing in the court. It is *never* the shot hit with the idea in mind that, "By God, this sucker's not coming back!"

THE BEGINNING STAGE

In the beginning of the point (serve and service return), the server has an easier job than the receiver as he may choose to start the point any way he wishes, hopefully to his advantage. For example, serving with the score tight and the momentum in the balance is not the time to showcase a cannonball. Nor is it the time for a whiffle ball accompanied by a prayer that the opponent will err. A high-percentage shot would be a three-quarter speed serve placed deep and *down the middle* since a wide serve gives the receiver a better opportunity to hit a sharply angled return. If you are the receiver on a very important point, now is not the time to be a hero and unleash a down-the-line passing shot in hopes of grabbing the point quickly while no one is looking. Stick to your "bread and butter," which should be a short-angled crosscourt. If, however, the speed, spin or height of the serve is suddenly more than you bargained for, don't stubbornly stick to a plan that is no longer likely to succeed. Recognize the emergency and use a defensive lob. If you play the deuce court and your right-handed partner is in the ad court, consider that an excellent high-percentage play is a deep lob into the alley behind the net player—the server's partner. (See diagram 9.) After the lob, move to the second volley position and be prepared to allow your partner to hit what will almost always be an easy overhead off your opponent's defensive lob. If your partner is a leftie and plays the deuce court, you can create the same situation for him by using an offensive lob from the ad court.

Remember, the goal is to reach the middle of the point and that is not possible if you don't get your service return in play.

THE MIDDLE STAGE

Once you reach the middle of the point, both of you must realize that your distance from the net and your opponents' court positions dictate your targets and responsibilities. The middle of the point can become frantic, allowing little time for quick decisions, and not knowing the proper direction in which to hit the ball can cause unforced errors.

Determining where to place shots, and in which direction during the middle or at the

Diagram 9
The Deep Lob: A High-Percentage Play

The deuce court player should utilize the offensive lob as a service return. Be sure to follow it to the net, allowing your ad court partner to prepare to smash the overhead.

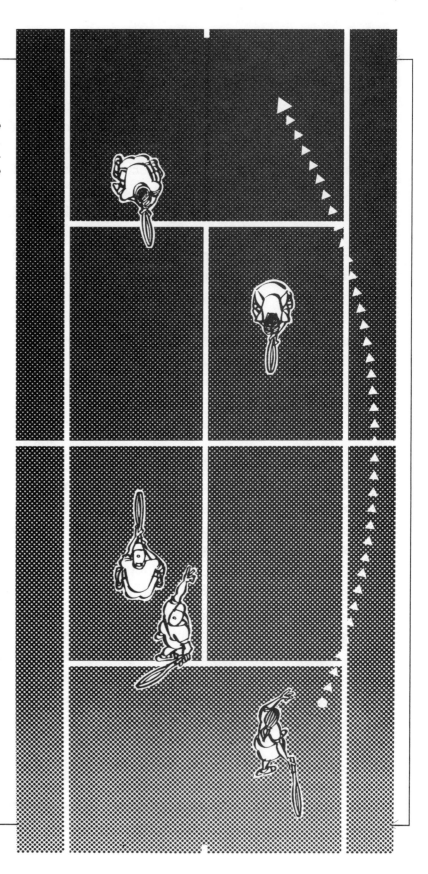

end of a point can be condensed into the Deep to Deep, Short to Short Axiom. (See diagram 10.) Doubles teams lose more points because of their failure to understand or implement this formula than they do for all other reasons combined. The four rules of this axiom are:

1. *Never* play a ball "deep to short."
2. *Always* play balls "deep to deep."
3. Play balls "short to short" whenever you can hit down and punish the "short" opponent, overheads included.
4. Play balls "short to deep" to keep your team out of trouble when hitting down is not an option.

The Deep to Deep, Short to Short Axiom will remove the tendency to hesitate and think about where the ball should be played—a prime reason easy volleys are misplayed. "Deep to deep" will keep you out of trouble and "short to short" will end the point for you at the proper moment. This axiom is fully explained in the diagrams on pages 38-39.

AIM FOR THE RIGHT TARGETS

What if both opponents are camped on their service line? What if all four of you have gained second volley position? Deep *people* and short *people* are not targets, nor are their racquets. The "deep-short" rules are only directional cues to indicate which targets on the court are appropriate in a given situation. "Short to short," "down the middle," "down the line," "deep to deep" are all direc-

tions, within which there are targets. No matter how well you crunch your "short to short" volley, if you hit a good player's racquet, the ball will come back—often over your head for a clean winner.

Playing high-percentage tennis is not just having the ability to choose the proper direction, but also having the ability to accurately strike targets within that direction. First of all, the primary target is *always* the grass, clay or asphalt, i.e., the *ground* on the other side of the net, not anything a player wears or carries. Bearing that in mind, there are only two possible targets for your first volley: either the ground just in front of the other "deep," usually cross court player's Nikes or down the middle to the "T." Your choice of target should be predicated on whether you must play the inside ball or the outside ball.

The Outside Ball

If you are a right-handed player executing a first volley (the first one for your team following return of serve) from the deuce court, your forehand volley is the outside ball and should be played crosscourt to the ground in front of your deep opponent's shoes, wherever they may be positioned. (See diagram 12.) It is doubtful that this wide volley could be played down the middle without encountering the net player's racquet.

The Inside Ball

If you must play a backhand volley, this is considered the inside ball and can be aimed

Diagram 10
The Deep to Deep, Short to Short Axiom

Where to direct and place shots during the middle or at the end of a point is easily summed up in this axiom: Always play your shots from "deep to deep," never "deep to short." Play your shots from "short to short" if you can hit down on them. (This includes overheads.) If hitting down on the ball isn't an option, play it "short to deep" to stay out of trouble. Looking at the diagram at right, imagine that you, the server, are moving toward the net and are about to strike your first volley. Your partner is in second volley position. Across the net, the receiver's partner is holding second volley position but the receiver has chosen to remain near the base line. Both your partner and the receiver's partner are close enough to the net to be able to hit down on any ball having sufficient net clearance to do so; thus their court positions may be defined as "short." You, the server, as well as the receiver, are both far enough away from the net that hitting down on any ball, regardless of its height, will send it into the net (overheads are the exception). If your distance from the net precludes your hitting down on a high volley or any ball that has bounced, your court position may be defined as "deep." It is a cardinal sin to play a ball "deep to short" since you, in all probability, will be hitting your shot with a trajectory rising up to an opponent's racquet poised to hit down at your vulnerable partner.

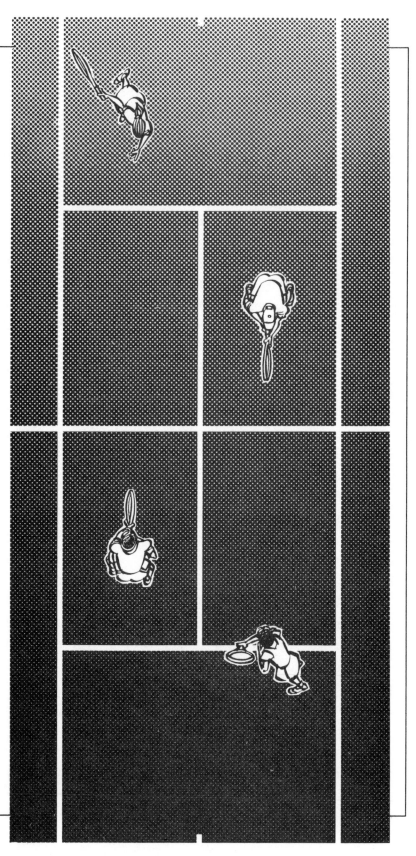

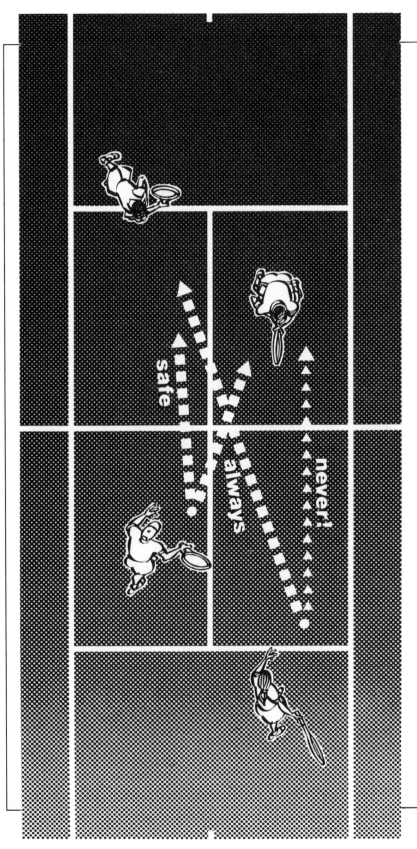

Diagram 11
Court Scenario: Ball Direction and Placement

The ad court player in the foreground is in a short court position. He may safely play low balls back in the direction from which they have come ("short to deep") in order to keep his team out of trouble. He should punish high balls by playing them toward the opposing net player ("short to short") who will have very little time to react. He will be guilty of not ending a point in a timely fashion if he plays a high ball toward the opponent who is farther from the net (inappropriate time for the "short to deep" selection).

The deuce court player in the foreground is in a deep court position. His only option is to play all of his balls in the direction of the opponent who is farther from the net ("deep to deep"). If he has a mental lapse and hits toward the short opponent, his partner might be maimed for life and should divorce him. (Never play a ball "deep to short.")

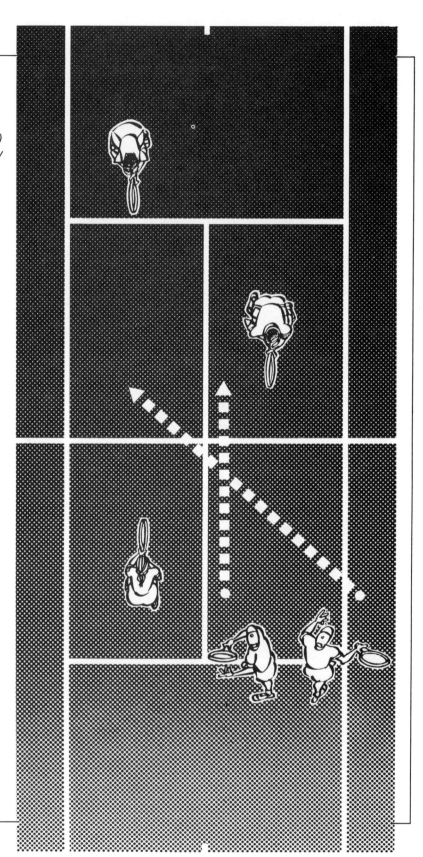

Diagram 12
Playing Inside and Outside Balls
The deuce court player should hit his forehand volley (the outside ball) crosscourt, and his backhand volley (the inside ball) through the middle of the court.

safely down the middle because it has no angle and will not cross the plane of the net player before it hits the ground. (See diagram 12.)

Remember that half-volleys are perfectly legitimate shots for either ball and are always preferable to an out-of-balance lunge to keep the ball from bouncing. If for some reason you are not in a position to hit either of these shots well, if your sixth sense tells you that you are having an emergency, lob the net player. Never panic, abandon ship, and offer up a wounded duck to the opposition in hopes that they will blow an easy setup. That only works when your opponents are absolutely incompetent.

Lastly, and this is true on all shots, but is particularly applicable to first volleys (where a "deep to short" shot will lose you the point), never get *cute*, *bored* or *stupid*. Adhere to the rule I impose on my students: "No CBS." The wee bit of court in the big guy's alley and the cute little piece of line on the extreme angle from you lying two inches beyond the net are the purview of rash fools.

OTHER TARGETS TO AIM FOR

Having successfully executed a first volley and gained second volley position, more options are available because of your proximity to the net. As shown in diagram 13, you have four targets available to you: one in each alley, about halfway between the imaginary extension of the service line and the net; one at the "T"; and one near the center mark dividing the base line.

If both of your opponents are in second volley position, you may choose any one of the front three targets, bearing in mind that it is always safest to pick the target most accessible to your racquet. (See diagram 13.) With all players in this formation, do not try to hit to the target near the base line because the ball will be too high as it moves between your opponents and will likely be cut off. Reserve this deep target for a time when a wide enough chasm exists in the center of the court and makes reaching a ball down the middle impossible for either opponent. Remember, the ball must hit the ground, and if it doesn't, you give your opponent an opportunity to put you in the most annoying of all predicaments—vulnerable to the dreaded lob-volley.

Whenever you observe that one opposing player is deeper in the court than another, even if by only a few steps, let your "deep to deep," "short to short" formula guide you in your selection of a target.

If you find that both of your opponents are positioned behind the base line, do not let the formation distract you. Realize that you no longer need to hit a crosscourt first volley because there are now two pairs of shoe tops exposed across the net. You may now play your first volley in whichever direction seems easiest, gain second volley position and prepare to hit down to one of the

Diagram 13
Playing From Second Volley Position
Both players may choose any of the three forward targets for their volleys, but they will reserve the deep target for a time when there is a wide rift between their opponents.

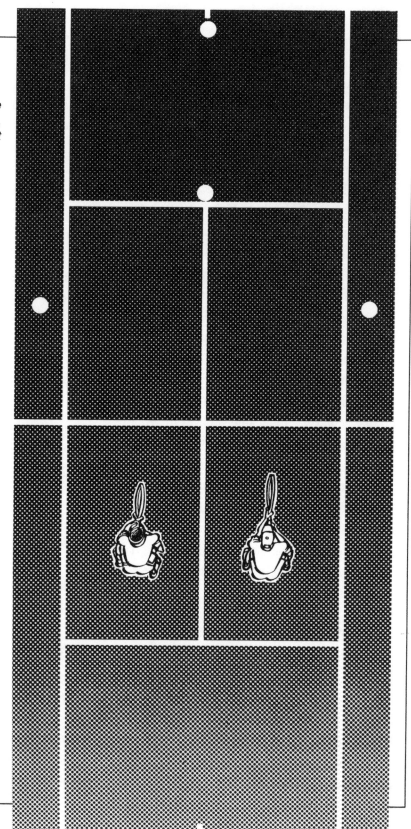

three front targets as soon as you receive a ball high enough to allow it.

POACHING THE BALL

At any time in a point you are free to cross in front of your partner and intercept or "poach" a ball (be sure to move forward on the diagonal—not laterally!). When you make this move, never choose the target lying in the alley on the side of the court you have just vacated. This error is called "hitting behind yourself," moving in one direction and playing the ball back in the direction from which you came. (See diagram 14.) An alert opponent will swiftly pick the ball up and send it down the line into the alley you have abandoned and which your partner has had no time to cross behind you and cover. If you meet up with the ball in the center of the court, choose the target at the "T." If you have passed the center of the court by the time you intercept the ball, choose the target in the alley toward which you are moving. Chapter five discusses poaching skills at length.

Closing the Net

"Closing the net" allows you to utilize sharply angled volleys and play your shots into parts of the court unavailable to you even from second volley position. The trick is to recognize when that option is present and to immediately take advantage of it.

Not long ago I was teaching a lesson in which the students were asked to recognize the soft, floating ball and instantly smother it by closing the net. The lesson was not going well. Exasperated, I finally asked, "For heaven's sake, what *is* a 'floater,' anyway?" One of the women timidly replied, "Well, I think it's a ball that used to be something else."

Although she was not completely accurate, this woman *did* have the right idea. Most balls that are mishit (struck off the frame or "dug out"), and therefore carry unintentional spin, end up "floating" across the net. Also, balls hit when a player is forced into a very awkward posture will often float.

You must learn to recognize floaters not only by watching your opponent's racquet, but by listening for that off-center sound of the mishit ball. Once you identify that juicy opportunity, close on the ball quickly and take advantage of your court position by rifling your volleys at extremely sharp angles. This move will not only allow you to play balls toward your alley targets, but your proximity to the net will give you the opportunity to hit a piece of ground well in front of the target. (See diagram 15.)

MAKING LOW-PERCENTAGE TENNIS PAY OFF

Low-percentage tennis can be defined as hitting shots that disregard the most appropriate speed, spin or direction for a given situation. Instead, a player selects a target or a racquet speed that allows far less margin for error but carries the element of surprise.

Diagram 14
Avoid Hitting Behind Yourself
Never move to the right and play your volley to the left, or vice versa. If you hit "behind yourself," an alert opponent will take the ball down your line for a winner.

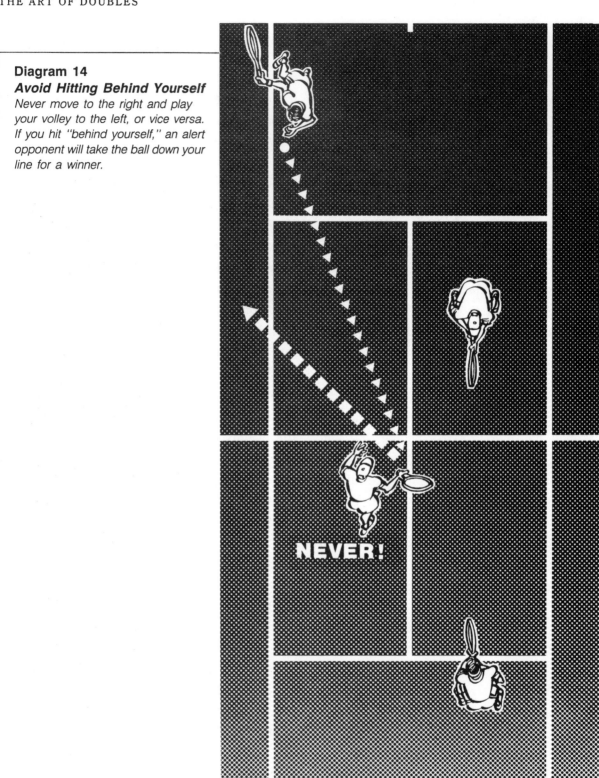

NEVER!

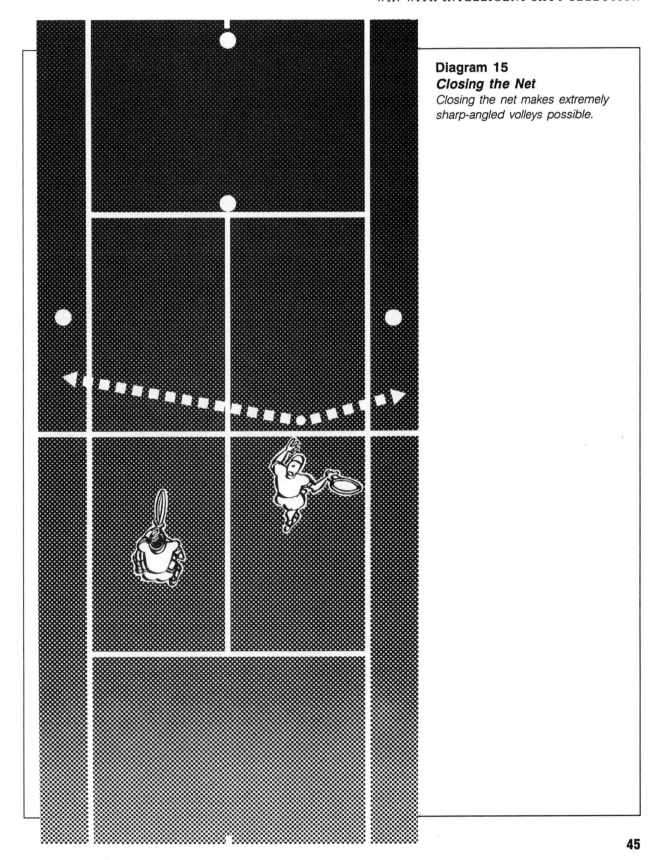

Diagram 15
Closing the Net
Closing the net makes extremely sharp-angled volleys possible.

In certain situations the psychological edge gained by successfully executing these low-percentage shots is worth the risk.

If yours is the receiving team and the server is down 0-40, it is an excellent time to unveil the most powerful service return in your arsenal. You may not have the confidence to unleash it at any other time in the match, but your opponents won't know that and will begin to wonder what you might hurl at them next.

Using low-percentage shot selection doesn't win matches, but it does make statements. When you are receiving serve at ad-out, the server is facing break-point. He may double fault and lose his serve, for which he has only himself to blame, but if he *does* give his service game away, he also knows that winning it the next time is within his power. If, on the other hand, you, as the receiver, cause him to lose his serve by surprising him with a superb low-percentage lob volley for a winner, or a softly angled volley that wrong-foots him, he may well feel incapable of ever controlling his service game again.

Executing a high-risk shot successfully is not only a wonderful confidence builder for your team, but also a morale destroyer for your opponents. Great doubles players know when the time is right and will not hesitate to try a very difficult shot, even in a tie-breaker. Bear in mind that a tiebreaker is designed to be close, and you should not panic if you fail to leap to a 6-0 lead. If you find yourself receiving serve at 5 points all in a tiebreaker, you should consider this a good time to surprise your opponents with your guts and courage by trying to make a clean winner. If you make it, your team serves for the set on the very next point. If you miss it, you are still "on serve" and should work hard to hold both your service points. Meanwhile, you have probably scared your opponents to death with your ability to be courageous under pressure.

KNOW WHEN TO BAIL OUT OF A SHOT

Experienced doubles teams know when to pressure their opponents with low-percentage shot selection, when to play high-percentage tennis and, just as important, when to bail out. What may seem like an intelligent choice of shots when you are balanced and poised to strike is always a bad idea if you suddenly find that your body is not centered over your feet. Differentiate between risk-taking, which has a reasonable probability of success, and failing to bail out, which has virtually no probability of success. If you plan to hit your service return down your opponent's line in a most convincing manner, but suddenly find the serve unexpectedly forcing, your original idea is no longer plausible. Rather than stubbornly sticking to it, you should immediately bail out, choosing instead to play a defensive lob. Failure to do so is not high-risk tennis. It is mindless disregard for an emergency.

Using high-risk shots when you are not playing well is a formula for disaster. If you can't make the routine "vanilla" shots on a given day, you most certainly won't make the high-risk shots. It might take longer, but stick patiently to your high-percentage arsenal.

Resist the temptation to be a hero. If the situation calls for a high-percentage safe volley, make it. Don't let the dreams of cheers and applause for the unbelievably impossible winner cloud your vision. Above all, learn to be comfortable with the knowledge that the end of the point is simply the one ball that you expected to come back, but didn't. Your team will truly have arrived when you begin to view the last ball as a disappointment rather than a relief.

Finally, don't get cute, bored, stupid, stubborn, fancy or greedy. Webster defines *intelligent* as "having knowledge, understanding and awareness." A truly intelligent doubles team must have all of that, tinged with generous doses of discretion and patience.

Shot Selection Checklist

✔ Play the beginning, the middle and the end of each point in order.

✔ Remember that mistakes you make in the beginning of a point are generally due to an unwillingness to play a long point.

✔ Mistakes you make in the middle of the point are often caused by not understanding the Deep to Deep, Short to Short Axiom (see page 37).

✔ Mistakes you make while trying to end the point are a result of not knowing where the targets on the court lie (see diagram 13).

✔ Use low-percentage, high-risk shots intelligently and only when the tenor of the match allows it.

✔ Make high-percentage tennis the rule, not the exception.

✔ Don't ever get CBS: cute, bored or stupid.

CHAPTER FIVE

Develop Superior Poaching Skills

It is only by risking our persons from one hour to another that we live at all. And often enough our faith beforehand in an uncertified result is the only thing that makes the result come true.

William James

Sometimes the word "poaching" itself is enough to make my students break into cold sweats. When I give a lesson on this technique, the idea is usually met with sheepish grins, but in the students' eyes I read, "Oh my God, you're going to make me risk looking like a fool, and maybe I'll do it in this lesson to humor you, but you'll never catch me running across the net and putting my partner's ball in the bottom of the net in a match." Sometimes in their determination to conquer their fear of poaching, or "taking a partner's ball," they career across the net so fast they end up interrupting a point on the court next to my teaching court, unable to put on the brakes in time.

Sometimes they have to listen to their own recalcitrant servers admonish from behind them, "You know, if you ever took my ball in a match, I'd kill you." Sometimes they start to move across the net, swing wildly at the ball, change their minds and retreat, after which they make a circle, turn around to see if their partners are there to play all and, ultimately, throw up their hands and appeal to me in utter confusion.

A great poacher is the most intimidating force a receiver can face, but making the move takes courage. Knowing when and how to move, and where to hit the ball, are skills of some intricacy.

If you and your partner choose *not* to be

A GREAT POACHER IS THE MOST INTIMIDATING FORCE A RECEIVER CAN FACE, BUT MAKING THE MOVE TAKES COURAGE, AND KNOWING WHEN AND HOW TO MOVE AND WHERE TO HIT THE BALL ARE SKILLS OF SOME INTRICACY.

a signaling team (the advantages and disadvantages of signaling your poaches are discussed later in this chapter), then you, when playing the net, can become a menacing freelancer whose movement can destroy your opponent's ability to return serve.

PLAN TO POACH

Just as your partner prepares to serve, assume your fierce posture and decide, *before the serve is struck*, whether you intend to poach even though you will only cross if the serve is hit down the middle. Make this decision before the ball is served because you must honor your wall responsibility and move laterally to cover the middle if you are *not* going to poach. Players think of this court

adjustment as a poach, but it is not. It is part of your obligation to mirror the placement of the ball according to the Wall Axiom. Having made this adjustment you will see that service returns coming directly over the center netstrap are yours to play. You may not refuse them. However, if you *have* decided to poach, you need not make the wall move. It is superfluous.

If you decide to poach, be alert to the placement of the serve. If it is wide and pulls the receiver toward your alley, you must immediately abort your plan in favor of the Wall Axiom, which indicates you must cover your alley. (See diagram 16.) However, if the serve is placed down the middle, you are in business. Begin your movement, forward on the

Diagram 16
Be a Patient Poacher
Wide serves are not good serves to poach on. Wait for or encourage your partner to serve either at the body or straight down the middle so that you can safely leave your alley un-protected.

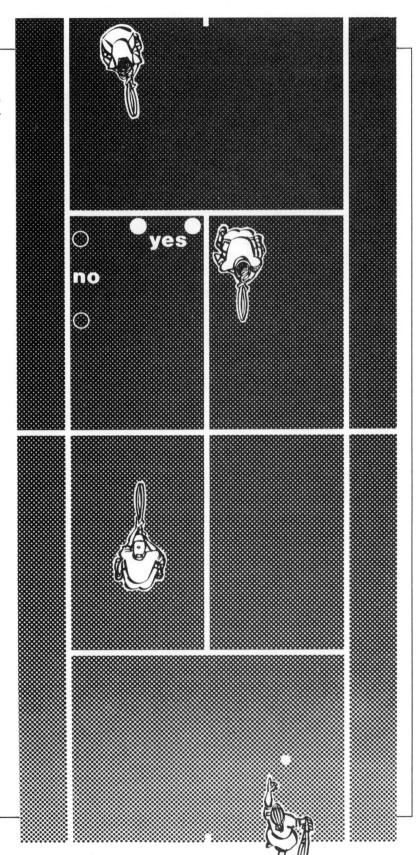

diagonal, as the receiver's eyes drop to the ball and his racquet starts forward. It is at this instant, having taken just a few steps, that the timid player loses heart and fears making an error in his partner's court.

The key to brilliant poaching is to realize that, as long as the move is not a signaled poach, you are under no obligation to go flying across the court into your partner's alley just because you begin to move. When you leave, you have no idea how low, hard, wide or high the ball will be, and it is absolutely not a mistake to change your mind and retreat. In fact, it is often prudent. The real mistakes are to go lurching wildly into your partner's court or to stop dead square in your partner's line of sight and turn around to look at him instead of getting out of the way.

REASONS TO ABORT A POACH

Here are several legitimate reasons to stop your move in midflight and quickly side-step back into your original position:

• If, having begun your poach, you see that the ball is hit hard and is headed for your partner's alley, you probably would never catch up with it. You should retreat.

• If you have crossed into your partner's court and find that when the ball reaches you it is approximately net level or below, step away and let the ball go through to your partner, who should have an easier play by virtue of his distance from the net.

• If your opponents play your partner's serve very early and from very close to the service line, it may also be taken on the rise. In this case, too, you should retreat because you have no time to react to the ball.

• In general, withdraw from balls sharply angling away from you, balls hit so hard that you cannot react in time, and balls crossing the net too low to punish.

If you follow these guidelines, you will be highly successful in putting away those balls you do choose to intercept. Once you understand which balls you should take and which balls you should let go through to your partner, your movement will become confident and fluid and you can begin to improvise.

STRATEGIES FOR POACHING

• Imagine that your partner serves wide to the player in the ad court. Having first discharged your wall responsibility by covering your alley, you realize that while the service return is angling away from you, it is a slow-moving, high "sitter." Go get it! The speed and height of the ball present no problems for you, so the floater can belong to you if you want it. A great poacher will always want it.

• Suppose the player in the deuce court returns serve so well that you have yet to get your racquet on one of his returns. Ask your partner to hit a wide serve. Then, try feigning a rather disinterested posture to make the receiver believe you have lost concentration. Just *before* the player prepares to strike his return, make a fake move to poach and immediately move to cover your alley. Many times this ploy will draw an attempt to pass you in your alley, for which you are absolutely prepared. Don't forget to smile as you volley a winner between your two stunned opponents.

• Another successful tactic employed by excellent poachers is to vary the starting court position. The first thing a receiver does when he prepares to return serve is note the server's partner's court position. Eliminate two of the receiver's service return options by positioning yourself close enough to the service line to discourage the lob and near enough to your alley to prevent a down-the-line shot. Your stance will often generate the crosscourt return you are looking to poach. If you do assume this position, adjust forward and to the center of your court as soon as you hear your partner serve. Otherwise, you will have too much court to cover for a successful poach. Remember that this position is a fake, assumed only to encourage the receiver to hit the shot you want him to hit.

• Similarly, if you begin the point with your nose hanging over the net, you are encouraging the lob—an excellent kind of fake for those who love to hit overheads. Again, remember to adjust out of your fake as you hear the serve being struck.

Constant variety in starting court positions is an advantage because the tactic tends to drive receivers crazy. Invent your own ways of distracting and otherwise harassing the receiving team. It is one of the most satisfying aspects of good doubles.

WHERE TO HIT A POACH

Knowing *where* to hit your poaches is just as important as knowing *if* you should take the ball. All the great movement in the world is of no value if you do not execute your volley to a proper target, and playing the ball in the wrong direction on a poach is definitely grounds for your partner to divorce you.

Always play the ball in the direction you are moving to allow your partner ample time to cross behind you. If you meet up with the ball in the center of the court, play the volley down the middle to the "T" so that the ball hits the ground. If you have crossed the center service line, choose the target in the alley toward which you are moving. Keep in mind that the closer you are to the net when you hit the ball, the more likely you will be successful. If you have begun your move on a serve to the deuce court opponent, your target is your ad court opponent's alley; if you began moving on the ad court opponent, your target is your deuce court opponent's alley. (See diagram 17.) Remember that the targets are in the respective opponent's alleys on the ground—*not* the sweet spots of their racquets. While it is true that occasionally you can hit hard enough at a player to intimidate him, good doubles players will not flinch and will often volley off your poach for a winner. Don't tempt fate. Ask yourself how hard is "hard enough" if your opponents are Navratilova and Shriver. *Never* poach a ball behind

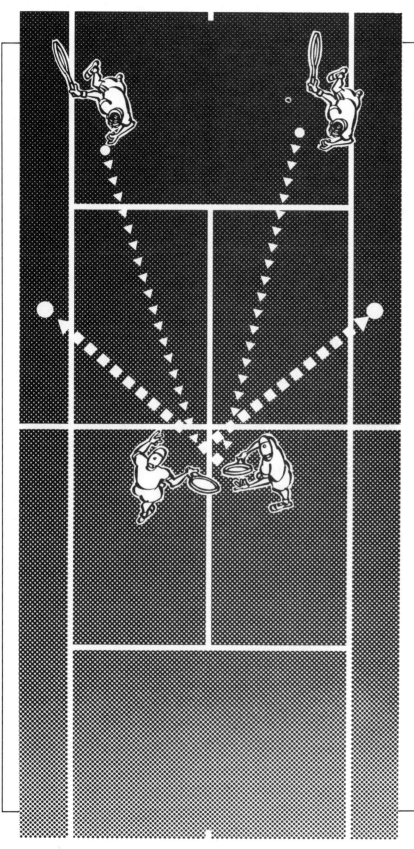

Diagram 17
Targets for Poaching
If you poach from the deuce court, your target lies in the deuce court opponent's alley. If you poach from the ad court, your target lies in your ad court opponent's alley.

yourself, that is, back in the direction from which you have come. The receiver will pick it up and shove it right down the alley you have vacated and no one will be there—you've left and your partner hasn't yet had time to arrive.

HOW YOUR PARTNER FIGURES INTO A POACH

The role of the server as backup is just as important as that of the interceptor on a smooth and polished poaching team. What gives a poacher the confidence to move and retreat, to start and stop, knowing full well that his behavior can be distracting, is the certain knowledge that his backup is fully concentrating and is ready to play all balls, or, if necessary, to cross behind his partner. The server must not react to the first few steps of the poacher. He must not cross too soon because he will have to remain on his side to play the ball if it is hit too low, hard or wide for the poacher. Often the players will be in an "i" formation, with the poacher literally in front of his partner momentarily.

If the server must play the ball, he must:

1. Be quick-witted enough to assess whether a crosscourt volley is possible, since his partner may be blocking the shot.
2. Avoid hitting his partner by quickly deciding to play the volley down the center, even if he must play the "outside" ball (see chapter four).
3. Assume the poacher's second volley position if the poacher makes ball con-

tact. Always move forward on the diagonal—never laterally along the service line. (See diagram 18.)

TO SIGNAL OR NOT TO SIGNAL?

Using poaching signals is truly a good news/bad news proposition. My doubles partner and I experimented with signals for a year and ultimately decided that it took away much of our spontaneity and often made us feel "rooted" when we had given a "stay" signal. We now do not signal our poaches against tough opponents who have forcing service returns, but we *will* use them against teams that continuously lob us (for reasons explained in chapter six on covering lobs properly).

The mere fact of using signals usually serves to distract your opponents. When you, as the net player, assume your court position and give that first hand signal, you can fairly bank on the fact that the receiver's heart just skipped a beat. And if you can get the receivers to guess with your signals—"Let's see, that's two 'goes,' one 'stay,' I bet this is a 'go' so I'll try a return into the alley." By then they've forgotten how to return serve and are now just playing a game of Twenty Questions with you.

WHAT THE SIGNALS MEAN

A signaled "go" means that you are responsible to play all balls hit in the direction you are moving, up to and including the opposite alley. Unlike the nonsignaled move, you

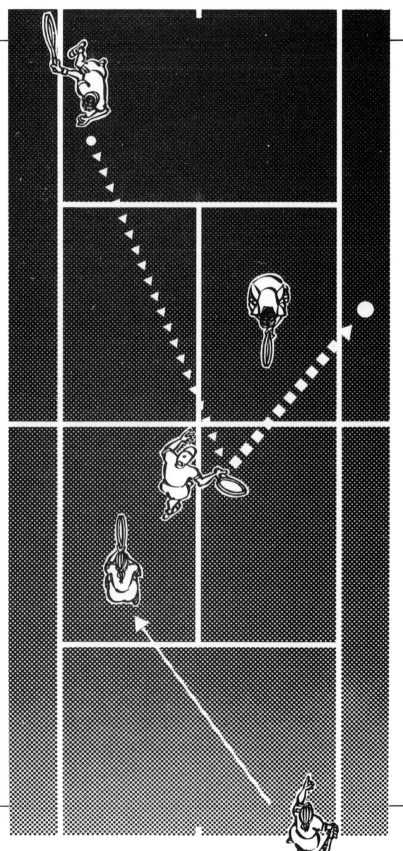

Diagram 18
The Server's Job When a Partner Poaches
If the poacher plays the ball, the server must quickly cross behind him and assume the second volley position vacated by the net player, making sure to move foward on the diagonal—never laterally.

must play the ball, no matter how hard, wide or low the return. In some cases you will be able to hit down to your target, ending the point. In some cases you must think of it as *starting* the point, taking care to play difficult low volleys back in the direction from which they came, or "blocking" hard-hit returns into the most accessible part of the court. Try not to be too ambitious for the situation, recognizing the difference between balls you can put away for winners and balls that must be handled carefully to avoid making an unforced error.

When signaling a "stay," be careful not to abdicate all responsibility for a ball whizzing by your ear. You still have your wall responsibilities and you should still be looking to poach a "wounded duck" return. You are still the player closer to the net until your server joins you and you must still look to intercept very weak returns. "Staying" does not mean total stagnation. It means being aware and alert.

As server, you always have the right to contradict the signal and ask for a different one. Since you should serve down the middle to make the move easier for your partner on all "go" signals, you would negate that "go" signal if you intended to serve wide on a particular point. If you are tired or out of breath and want help, refuse the "stay" by simply saying "no" and your partner should respond by flashing you the "go" (poach) signal that you are looking for.

When using signals, you, as the net player, may begin your move a second earlier than if it were a nonsignaled poach because your partner is automatically crossing behind you and the entire court should be covered. The server should take care to move forward on the diagonal, his goal being to assume the net position you have vacated. This is a difficult move for the server because he has a great deal of court to cover in order to position himself for the potential "down the line" return. For this reason, although serving "wide" is not a taboo when using signals, he should bear in mind that if he *does* serve "wide," he will have very little time to gain second volley position and nab a "down the line" return, which will reach his side of the court very quickly and without angle.

Another problem for the signaling team is the "down the middle" service return. Once the server has put the ball in play, there can be no change of plan when using signals. If you are a right-handed player moving across the net in a point served to the deuce court, you cannot halt your progress across the net, stop, and reach back to backhand volley since this freezes your team in an "i" formation and is tantamount to changing the plan. Your server, who expects you to be well across the center service line at this point, is poised to play the ball. If you change directions to stab at a volley, neither side of the court is covered and neither of you knows where to go next. As net player, you must have the discipline to let all balls hit behind you go through to the server and stick to the plan, which is that your movement across the net is continuous and should not be interrupted. (See diagram 19.)

HOW TO SIGNAL

Many players use a clenched fist behind the back for a "stay" signal and an open palm for a "go" signal, resignaling between first and second serves when the first serve is a fault. As a server, I find this distracting and prefer my partner to use one signal per point—one finger pointed down if he is only going on the first serve, two fingers pointed down if he intends to go on both serves, or the clenched fist if he is "staying." In all cases, the server must verbally acknowledge the signal before serving or the net player cannot be sure the server knows which play has been called. When accepting your partner's signal, always use the same words and tone of voice, no matter which signal has been given. Two of my students came to me not long ago and complained that their poaches never really worked because it seemed that somehow the opponents *always* knew whether they were "going" or "staying." After much investigation we discovered that when one of the team members was the server, she would acknowledge her partner's "stay" signal with a simple "Yea," uttered without enthusiasm, and she answered her partner's "go" signal with a highly animated "Oh-kay!"

Using poaching signals is definitely more difficult than freelancing volleys. Unlike the spontaneous move, the signaled poach is an irrevocable commitment to cross the net. Signaling will often help the reluctant net player, who would otherwise never venture forth, to experiment with uncharted territory, but it also forces the player into making some very difficult volleys. On the other side of the question, freelancing requires a great many last-second decisions, and players who are inexperienced or who do not trust their judgment will sometimes end up not taking the balls they should.

Whether your team eventually decides on signaling or freelancing or a combination of both, it is vital to your team's ability to hold serve that you *do* poach because the intimidation factor alone is beyond measure. Think about the last time you played a team that moved a great deal on your service returns. Do you actually remember how many they made and how many they missed? Or do you just remember wishing like hell that they would stand still so you could return serve? Many of my students are so worried about leaving their alleys uncovered for a potential winner that they simply refuse to vacate their position—ever. Somehow they feel personally humiliated and defeated if they are passed in the alley. I wish they would feel equally as defeated when the lob sails over their heads. Anybody can, and will, make a winner. And if it happens to be one struck into your vacant alley, so be it. You don't even have to say "nice shot," or even notice the smirk across the net. Simply get on with your job,

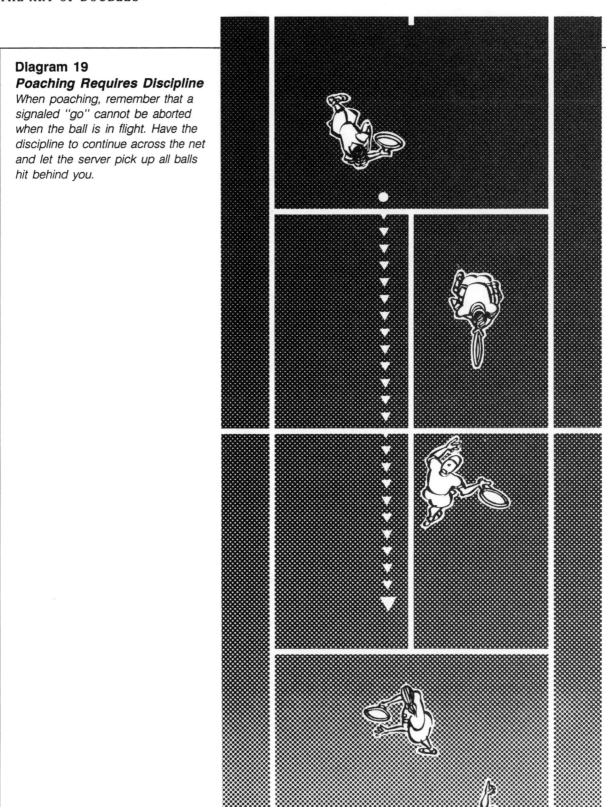

Diagram 19
Poaching Requires Discipline
When poaching, remember that a signaled "go" cannot be aborted when the ball is in flight. Have the discipline to continue across the net and let the server pick up all balls hit behind you.

and never let a passing shot or two deter you from poaching. The rewards are definitely worth the work it requires to become a good poaching team. And if, in the end, you still do not feel comfortable taking "your partner's ball," remember that any time you cross in front of your partner to play a shot, you cut off your opponents' recovery time substantially, *and* you create a new and better angle for your volley.

Poaching Checklist

✔ Great poachers make winning the service game easy for the server.

✔ The key to good poaching skills is having discretion, knowing which balls to play and which to leave.

✔ Know which targets to aim for.

✔ The server, or backup, must understand how crucial he is to the overall success of a poaching team.

✔ Use signals to confuse your opponents but back the signals up with excellent volleying skills.

✔ Do not use signals if you prefer to preserve the spontaneity of the move. Know the trade-off, though—hesitant poachers will remain just that.

✔ Remember that half of the value of poaching is to intimidate the receiver.

CHAPTER SIX

Keeping Control of the Net

*Excellence is achieved. It is not stumbled upon
in the course of amusing oneself. It is built upon
discipline and tenacity of purpose.*

Racquet Quarterly Magazine

I feel very sorry for some of my students because, if I am to believe what they tell me, they are never the recipients of short lobs. It appears that all "lob queens" reserve their deepest and finest for these poor students, and each time they come off the court they unfailingly assure me that every single lob their opponents hit definitely bounced *on* the base line. And, of course, any time the ball bounces behind you on the court, you must relinquish the net and play defense. Matches can be won by defending the court from behind the base line, or by playing "one up, one back," for that matter. But neither of these formations can make a dent in the armor of a team possessing supe-rior volleying skills whose expertise extends to maintaining control of the net and not losing it in the face of a barrage of lobs. The only way to establish a pattern of consistent success in doubles is to learn to take the net immediately on every point and keep it by not allowing lobs to bounce behind you.

HANDLING THE DREADED SERVICE RETURN LOB

The perception that *every* service return lob is "way too deep, way over my head, a ball my partner must cover for me," is a common one, but it is an exaggeration born of a player's unwillingness to accept responsibility for a ball traveling over his own head.

Some lobs really are too deep for the net player to handle, and are more easily played by the server who has not yet reached second volley position. But the net player has the responsibility for that decision and should not automatically abdicate.

If you are the server's partner, you must remember that your server is coming to the net fully focused on his job, expecting to have to play a wide volley or to back you up if a ball returned up the middle is unpoachable. Chapter five on poaching mentions that the server must believe that all volleys are his to play unless pleasantly surprised. If, as the net player, you expect your partner to cover those volleys *and* be responsible for all service return lobs, then the question is: What are *you* doing out there?

If a lob is aimed over *your* head, it is *your* problem, and while there are times you are absolved from the responsibility of hitting the ball, *you* are the one who must make the decision by quickly and loudly saying either "Mine" or "Yours." It should never be the case that both players tacitly assume the server always bails his partner out by automatically crossing behind him and chasing the bouncing lob. Every time you handle a service return in this manner, you lose control of the net.

There are three ways—with difficulty levels of beginning, intermediate and advanced—for you, as server's partner, to turn those devastating lobs into easy overheads, and a way to maintain control of the net which involves teamwork between you and your server.

Beginning: Move to the Service Line

If you, the net player, are just learning to play the net and are not yet confident of your footwork or racquet-reading skills, you may worry that the impending service return may be a lob over your head. The simplest thing you can do to dissuade the receiver is to reposition yourself on the service line before the ball is served. While this strategy is generally effective, it has drawbacks. First, if you stay there after the serve is hit, you are too far away from the net to cover the down-the-line return. Second, it is a rather fearful stance and sends the message to your opponents that you cannot cover a lob without a head start. It may set the stage for more mid-point lobs than might have otherwise occurred. It is better to discourage "lob queens" with a very confident demeanor that is sprinkled with a cocky bit of "I don't care if you lob; I have an overhead."

Intermediate: Guess-and-Go Move

A method of displaying that kind of cocky confidence, albeit perhaps totally false, is guessing with the receiver. Have you ever had that prickly little feeling that means, "I just know this will be a lob"? If you have just successfully poached two balls in a row, isn't a lob a good bet? In this situation, maintain your normal second volley position, but when the serve *lands* on the other side of the net, turn around and run, with racquet prepared to hit an overhead. By leaving the starting block this early you will reach even the deepest lob in time to play an aggressive overhead. The beauty of the move is that the receiver will not know that you only guessed. He will think you have an uncanny ability to read his racquet preparation almost before it starts and will be quite discouraged. If, in making this move, you find that you have guessed wrong, nine times out of ten the return will be a crosscourt, for which you are not primarily responsible anyway, and you will have lost nothing. Just pull your racquet down and return to second volley position. Never feel like an idiot for having made a false move. Remember that the receiver cannot tell that you are guessing and is more likely to think you saw something in his racquet preparation that made you react as if it were a lob. He is far more likely to credit your perspicacity than he is to criticize your imbecility.

The guess-and-go move should be used as an interim step if you are an intermediate player who has not yet developed sufficient racquet-reading skills to be able to *see* the lob coming. The best doubles players anticipate the lob by watching their opponents' racquets diligently and gliding gracefully into position just as the ball is being struck on the other side of the net. These advanced players enjoy taking their own lobs and enjoy knowing that they cannot be stampeded off the net by the lobbers.

Advanced: "Read" the Opponent's Racquet

Anticipating the return by "reading" the racquet is the most sophisticated method of covering a lob, but it is a skill acquired over time. To the eternal frustration of many, there are no shortcuts. You cannot buy this skill from a tennis teacher, as you might a topspin serve. It is an experiential process of trial and error, and after an indeterminate number of years of racquet-watching, what once seemed so obscure will become obvious. A subtle tilt of the racquet face, a drop of the racquet head, a change in racquet preparation will instantaneously drive your feet into action and you will be in position to hit the overhead even before the ball arrives. Once developed, this skill frees you from feeling that you are at the mercy of the dreaded lobbers.

Use the Signaled Poach to Control the Net

Finally, the serving team can maintain control of the net in the face of a service return lob by using the signaled poach (see chapter five). My partner and I find the signaled poach to be an excellent weapon against teams whose only goal is to drive you off the net by lobbing almost every service return.

When faced with a situation in which receivers are lobbing service returns consistently, use your hand signals and signal the "go" at least four out of five times. Then you, as the net player, should cross the net and get out of the way of the lobbed return. Your serving partner, who has crossed behind you, will play it as a high volley on his way to the net. (See diagram 20.) Even as you move out of the path of the ball, be alert to the possibility that the return is a crosscourt and thus *your* ball. The server will often be faced with a difficult volley and must take care not to overhit his shot, choosing instead to play the ball safely toward the receiver—the person farther from the net. While this strategy does not involve the most aggressive play on the lob—that is, the server's partner hitting the overhead smash—it nevertheless preserves the team's offensive court position and prevents relinquishing net control.

If, as the net player, you make a commitment to poach on a particular service return and your body is committed forward, you cannot reverse momentum in time to cover a lob. However, since that lob is technically yours, you must ask your partner for help by calling "Yours!" very quickly. Your server is a very busy person; don't expect him to do his job *and* read both your mind and your body language. Your partner should drift behind you, give the command "Stay!" and play the ball in the air. He should place his volley in the alley of the receiver who executed the lob. You *do not cross at the net* nor fade backward. Hold your side of the court and move in to become the "toe protector" (see page 27) until your partner recovers his side of the court and gains second volley position. (See diagram 21.) This play absolutely negates the effectiveness of the lob, maintains an offensive posture and keeps net control.

The only time this play does not work is if the lob really would bounce on the base line in your alley. In this case, if your partner tries to take the ball in the air, know that he simply cannot recover to his own side of the court before the opponent's return shot. On these rare occasions, your partner should issue the command "Back!" to you, bounce the lob, and lob the ball back across the net. (See diagram 22.) Meanwhile, you turn around and run diagonally to stand behind the base line. Your team has no choice but to play the rest of the point from the defensive court position. Most of the time, the lob can and should be taken in the air by the server. Teams that commit to keeping the net by *not* allowing balls to bounce except when absolutely necessary will find that many balls they have previously let bounce are perfectly playable in the air.

This play management distinguishes a great doubles team, which will *keep* the net, from the inexperienced team, which will tend to panic and flee.

DEFENDING AGAINST LOBS OTHER THAN SERVICE RETURNS

The offensive lob executed against your team in the middle of a point is a more difficult proposition, primarily because the ball can be aimed over *either* of your heads. Not only must you read that it is a lob, but you must also read its direction. In this situation you, as a team, cannot position yourselves on the service line in hopes of deter-

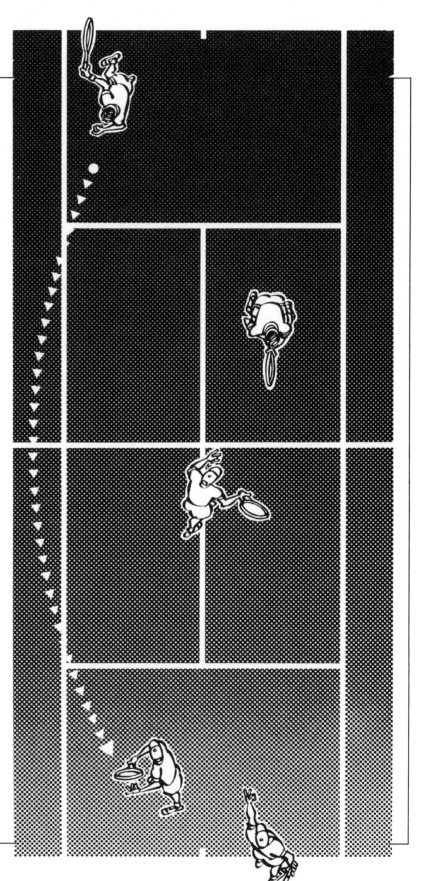

Diagram 20
Playing the Lobbed Return
As a prearranged plan, you, the server's partner, have moved across the net. Although you remain alert for a poach, you are really moving out of the way so that your serving partner can reverse directions and play the service return lob as a high volley on his way to the net.

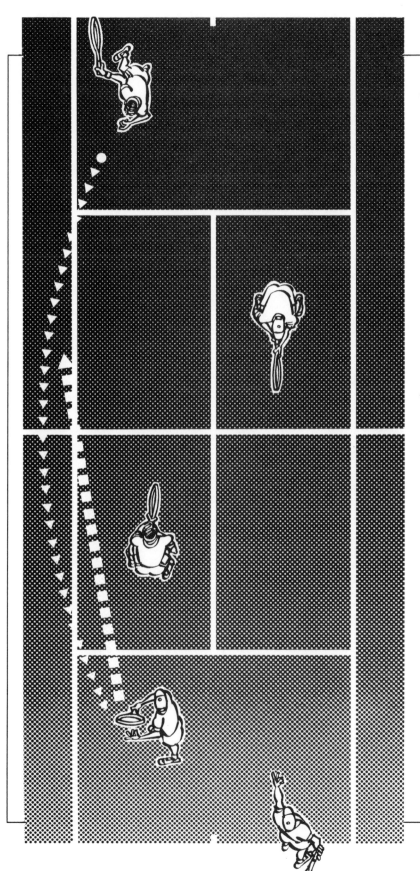

Diagram 21
***Another Way to Cover the
Service Return Lob***
*The server has taken the lob in the
air from behind his partner. He has
issued the command "Stay!" to the
net player and he will recover to his
own side of the court as soon as he
has executed his backhand volley off
the lob.*

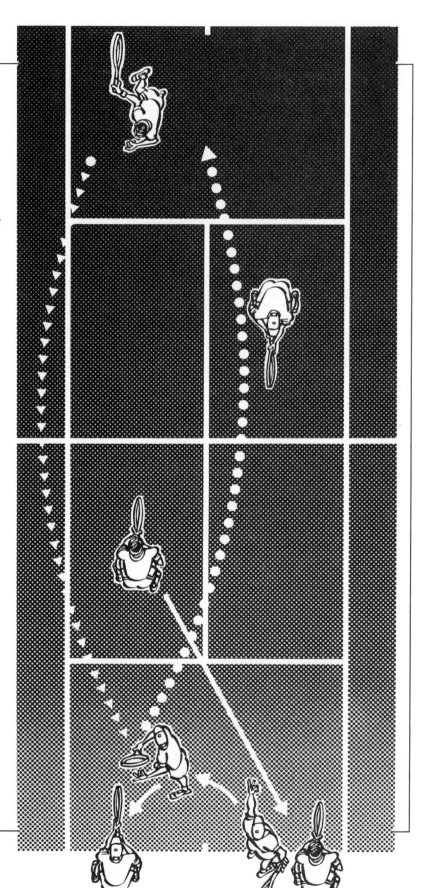

Diagram 22
When to Bounce the Lob

If the lob is simply too deep to be played effectively in the air and the server cannot gain his net position before the ball is returned by the opponent, he issues the command "Back!" to the net player, bounces the ball and lobs it back, and both players assume the defensive court position.

ring the lob because you cannot offensively volley the low ground stroke you have invited from that court position. Nor can you both "guess" lob and start running back to cover the ball before you are certain that it is, in fact, a lob. If you are wrong and the opponent has chosen a ground stroke, you are even more out of position for a volley than you would be waiting on the service line. Covering the lob successfully in the middle of a point is a function of your ability to anticipate what is coming and your knowledge of what a player can and cannot do with a ball from certain court positions. For this reason, it is difficult for inexperienced teams to maintain firm control of the net for an entire point.

Assume that you are well into a long point and have control of the net. Both of your opponents are positioned near the base line. In order to retain your second volley position, each of you must make sure that no lob gets over you and bounces, since that would send you both back to the base line and allow your opponents to claim the net. The only way to successfully control the net is to know in advance that a lob is coming and begin moving back to hit an overhead before the lob is even in the air.

You can force an opponent to hit a lob by sending him a deep volley that infringes upon his "timing space," the room and time he needs to prepare to hit a shot. If you volley very deep—to within several inches of his shoelaces—or if you volley deep and wide into his alley—sending him hurtling toward

the ball at a dead run—he no longer has his "timing space." (See diagram 23.) When your opponent has neither the room nor the time to choose his shot, he *must* lob, and since you know that, immediately upon executing a deep volley, your team should drift back expecting to hit an overhead. When you leave, you do not know how high, how deep, or over which of you the ball will travel, but you *do* know that to clear the net, it must be a lob. *Avoid* the temptation to close the net after volleying near the base line because even the short lob will land behind you.

If, in this same situation, you have not volleyed well, and your opponent still has his "timing space," you must rely on your anticipation and your ears to maintain your second volley position. Watch his racquethead carefully and react quickly to what you see, bearing in mind that it is wise to try to close the net if you read a ground stroke coming toward you because closing makes the volley easier to angle away from your opponent. If you are unsure what is coming, listen carefully. Very often the ball will be struck fractionally later if it is to be lobbed because it takes marginally longer to stroke that shot.

It is best to keep your team in a position to predict what is coming by volleying deep, putting your opponents on their heels and forcing them to hit what you know they must—a ball in the air. However, that is not always possible, and since your task is to keep control of the net, regardless of what your opponents throw at you, you must be

Diagram 23
The Value of Timing Space
The player in the deuce court has his timing space. He has the room and time he needs to execute any shot he chooses. The player in the ad court is on his heels. He has neither the room nor the time to choose his shot. Therefore, whether intentionally or not, his ball will rise as it clears the net.

DON'T ACCOMMODATE THOSE IRRITATING LOBBERS BY ALLOWING THEM TO OPERATE IN THEIR COMFORT ZONE, RETAINING THEIR TIMING SPACE. HIT DEEP ENOUGH TO PUT THEM ON THEIR HEELS OR MAKE THEM CHASE BALLS.

prepared for a great deal of movement and footwork on every point. It is likely that in any given point against good baseliners, you will have moved back for an overhead and in for a low volley, both individually and as a team, as many as four or five times. This is the only effective way of retaining your second volley position. Standing in one spot and hoping to lunge forward for a volley and reach back for an overhead just won't do it.

The service return lob can be kept from bouncing by your good teamwork and communication skills. The lob in the middle of the point is much more difficult to defend against. You must be able to keep the "lob queens" from choosing their weapons by volleying deep enough to make their lobs pre-dictable. While you cannot stop them from lobbing you entirely, you can control the net by making sure that your volleys elicit nothing but responses you can easily anticipate. If you volley poorly and give an opponent too much time, your movement is frozen while he chooses his shot and it becomes very difficult for your team to cover all of the various possibilities—lobs, passing shots, dink shots. Also, remember that you control the lob volley by making sure that your volleys hit the ground rather than a racquet.

If, as a serve-and-volley team, balls are flying over your head and bouncing consistently, the match is being played behind you, being dictated by the "lob queens," and it's a good bet that you're losing. "Oh, damn!"

is not an acceptable response to the lob, nor is standing around in stunned silence as the lob lands unplayed behind you for a winner. Further, every time your team scrambles for the base line, you elicit self-satisfied smirks from the lobbers across the net. They love watching the cattle stampede.

Be determined to read racquets, anticipate, hit forcing volleys and use good communication skills. Your efforts will be rewarded by the feeling that you are invulnerable to all efforts to force you to retreat and relinquish the net.

Net Control Checklist

- ✔ Remember that every time a ball bounces behind you, you must relinquish the net.

- ✔ Service return lobs can be covered in such a variety of ways that they should rarely bounce.

- ✔ Use forcing volleys to keep mid-point lobs from bouncing.

- ✔ Insuring that your own volleys hit the ground will put an end to lob volleys.

- ✔ Make a firm commitment with your teammate to play the ball in the air whenever possible in order to preserve your offensive court position and maintain net control.

- ✔ Every time you make the effort to read a racquet, boldly call "Mine," and execute the overhead smash. You will reinforce your declaration that you intend to dominate the net, and that you are invulnerable to all efforts to force you to retreat.

CHAPTER SEVEN

Understanding Your Jobs on the Court

*Life always gets harder toward the summit—
the cold increases, responsibility increases.*

Friedrich Nietzsche

I have been convinced for some time now that a fair number of the "watchers" and "wonderers" believe that certain court positions are more desirable than others in that they afford a player a chance to rest or, even better, hide. Timid players feel that they are absolved from the responsibility of actually hitting a tennis ball when occupying one of these "static" court positions, those of the server's partner and the receiver's partner. Some of my bravest students have come forward to confess that my long-held suspicions are indeed accurate. They plead guilty to chanting "Please, God, don't let the ball come to me" often enough that I fear it becomes some players' mantra—a creed not destined to great teamwork.

On the contrary, great doubles players know that these two court positions are more dynamic than those of server and receiver. They are keenly aware that what a player in one of these court positions does, or does not do, will determine the outcome of a point far more often than what the server or receiver does.

CONSIDER YOURSELF "ON THE JOB"

Many players have developed attitudes reminiscent of Melville's Bartleby the Scrivener about court positions. Faced with the prospect of having to perform duties they consider hazardous to their mental health, they, like Bartleby, simply dig in their heels and announce that they "would prefer not to." For this reason, I have described those actions of superior doubles players "jobs" on the court, in the hope of persuading doubters and "fearful Freddies" that compliance is an essential ingredient of success.

One aspect of a great doubles team is each player's ability to hit shots in consideration of his partner's job. If one player on a team keeps playing an entire point, something is very wrong. The great doubles player knows not only his own job, but that of his partner, and therefore unselfishly hits the shot that will enable his partner to enter the point and properly do his job without fear of failure or reprisal. Thus, if I serve down the middle, I know I need not cover the return coming through the center since my partner will, according to the axiom of the wall, position himself directly opposite the place the ball has landed.

The following "job descriptions" will help you understand the individual responsibilities a player has when occupying each of the four roles on the court. When both players execute their respective duties properly, the result is the choreographed smoothness and grace of true teamwork.

THE SERVER

Hold Serve is the first rule of good tennis, singles or doubles. In singles it's all up to you, but in doubles you should get a great deal of help from your partner. However, it is ultimately your responsiblity to win your service game. Remember that if you lose it, your opponents don't feel that they broke the *team*. They know that they broke *you*. Only one name is ever attached to a service break.

• Get your first serve in! Find a nice, consistent serve that is about 75 percent of the pace you have available to you. Your partner needs a rhythm to poach effectively, and nothing is so discouraging to that eager poacher as a string of false starts on your missed first serves.

• Approach the net shading toward the alley, no matter where you serve, so that you have a decent play on the low, wide returns. If you serve down the center, your partner will take the return coming straight back through the center, though you must not expect his help on low or hard balls angling away from him. Recognize that if you serve down the center, you and your partner have 80 percent of the court covered, leaving only your partner's alley unprotected. (See diagram 24.) If you serve wide, the wall says that your partner must protect the alley and that the center ball is yours to play on the diagonal although you must come to the net wide enough to cover the angled return. In this case you only have about 20 percent of the court well covered. (See diagram 25.)

• Don't be a "watcher" or a "wonderer" who insists upon serving "wide" to the ad court, assuming you have served "to the backhand." I have never understood this since it makes so many false assumptions.

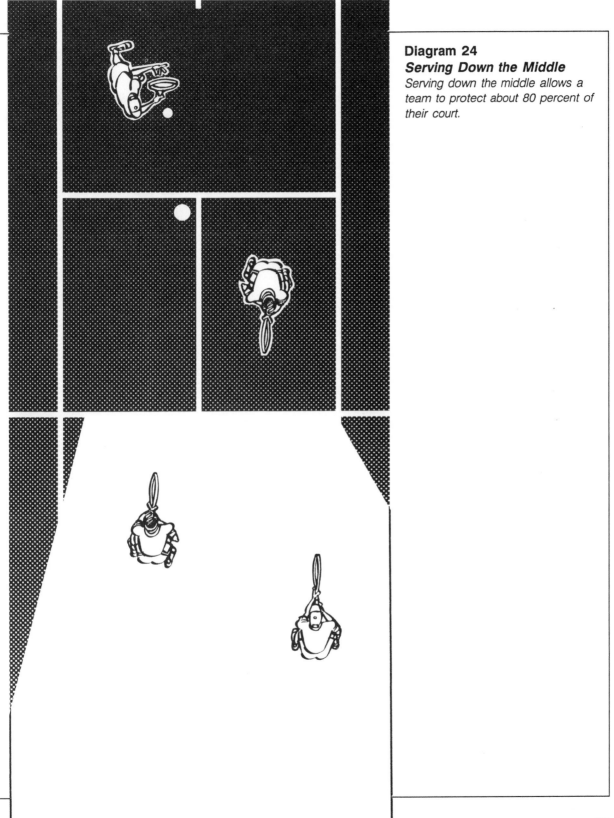

Diagram 24
Serving Down the Middle
Serving down the middle allows a team to protect about 80 percent of their court.

Diagram 25
Serving Wide

Serving wide divides a team's responsibilities and allows a receiver to hit into a great deal of unprotected court.

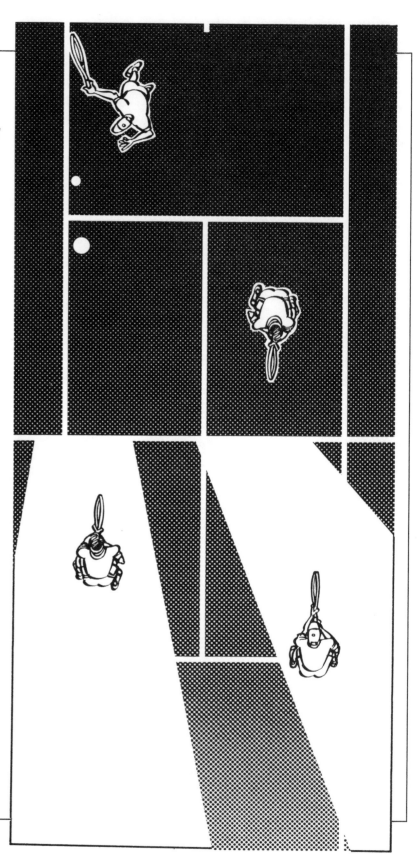

First, it assumes the world is right-handed. Second, it assumes the backhand is weaker. And third, it assumes it is okay to leave 80 percent of the court unprotected. Naturally, none of these assumptions are reasonable. In particular, covering only 20 percent of the court exerts little pressure on your opponent to be accurate.

• Believe that any service return over the net (except, perhaps, the lob in certain circumstances)—anywhere in the court—is yours to volley. Be delighted if your partner intercepts it for you. Even though you may know the information intellectually, it is difficult for the muscles to remember that your partner, at the net, *may* begin to move across the net, but may retreat, choosing not to play hard-hit balls angling away, low balls, or even some high balls hit hard enough that he has insufficient time to react.

• Never relax your racquet. Get your first serve in, hope your partner can put the ball away for you, but don't expect it. Be prepared to hit all balls, never allowing yourself to be distracted by your eager net player's movement.

• Never hurry your first volley. Take care to hit a good, low crosscourt on a wide service return, and a solid reply up the middle on a return aimed up the middle. Remember that if the ball bounces on your side of the net, it bounces. Half-volleys are perfectly acceptable. There is no value in your rushing your volley in order to prevent a ball from bouncing when prudence would dictate a half-volley.

THE SERVER'S PARTNER

In the position of server's partner, you have many responsibilities. This is not a time to rest and pray that the ball doesn't come to you. This is a time to play an active role in winning the service game. Imagine the following scenario:

Server places a first serve down the middle. Partner, who has chosen not to poach, fails to cover the middle. Service return is hit up the middle and falls good, unplayed. 0-15. Server serves an excellent serve (which he has communicated in advance to his partner) wide to the backhand of the player in the ad court. The receiver can do nothing but play a weak lob over the head of the net player. The net player says nothing and simply sashays to his ad court, remaining at the net. Server is caught unaware and has no play on the ball. 0-30. Server again serves a first serve down the middle. Net partner, determined to avenge all previous wrongs, darts across the court only to poach a ball much too low for a successful attempt, and, alas, places the ball in the bottom of the net. 0-40. Server, slightly unhinged and definitely feeling ragged around the edges, double faults. Game. Server's partner, if, in fact, he is still wanted as a member of this team, needs education.

• Your wall responsibilities take first priority. Watch carefully where the serve lands, remembering to "mirror" that spot on the court. If it is a wide serve, protect the alley; if it is down the middle, move to the center if you are *not* going to poach. (The move is superfluous if you intend to move across the net.)

• Remember that the height of a ball changes your targets. Don't try to change the angle of a low ball; return it in the same direction and do so "short to deep." If it is high enough for you to hit down on the ball effectively, return it to a target in the "short to short" direction.

• Distract the receiver and make him hit the shot *you* want him to play, not the shot that *he* wants to play. Draw the ball down your line by faking to the middle; invite an overhead by crowding the net; encourage a crosscourt by hugging your alley, and then poach it off. The more aggressive and fearless you are, the more frozen in fear the receiver becomes.

• Call "out" balls for your team since it is much more difficult for the on-rushing server to determine if he might be about to play an "out" ball.

• Be the verbal captain of your team, and "call the play." Don't be afraid to suggest a service placement that you feel will elicit a predictable response, or to ask for that wide serve so that you can execute your fake and tease the receiver into trying your alley. If your server is having trouble volleying that great low, wide crosscourt, it is your job to prompt him to try the Australian formation (see page 86 for an in-depth discussion of this).

• View this court position as one that will earn some free or easy points if you successfully draw the receiver's attention away from the ball and toward you. Be a bothersome distraction.

• Remember that movement and courage are the keys to playing this court position correctly. More service games are lost because of this player's inactivity than are ever lost by his activity.

THE RECEIVER

If you don't return serve, there is no service break, and if you don't break serve, you don't win matches. Returning serve successfully requires concentration, thoughtful planning and careful execution.

• Heroes need not apply. Be consistent, not flashy, and remember to hit shots in consideration of your partner's duties. Never become too predictable, sprinkling in a fair number of offensive lobs, a few balls at the net person, and an occasional passing shot down the line or through the middle.

• Stick to the shot that allows your partner to enter the point—the low, wide crosscourt that lands no deeper than the service line. A deep service return in doubles is a poor choice, unless you can give assurances that you can hit the base line. If the server rushes the net, the deep return is higher and easier to volley. If the server stays back, your "deep" return, which probably, in reality, lands two to three feet inside the base line, is right in his comfort zone. Sadly for you, he doesn't even have to move his feet to pass you, or worse yet, lob you on his next shot. Conversely, the low, wide service return is, as we all know, much more difficult to volley, and much more difficult for the baseline-hugger to reach.

• Plan the return in advance, realizing that if the serve is good enough to create an "emergency," that is, the planned return is no longer possible because of the speed, spin or placement of the serve, a defensive lob is the appropriate response. Players whose strength is their return of serve always know when they are having an emergency and do not foolishly stick to a plan that is no longer an option for those conditions, never allowing themselves to get too ambitious for the situation. If they can get their racquets on a ball, they put that ball in play using the defensive lob whenever necessary.

• Don't be a "watcher" or a "wonderer." Don't stand around admiring your return. Follow it to the net, bearing in mind that the center ball is yours on the diagonal. Even if the serve pulls you wide, if the server hits the next shot down the middle, it is *your* ball. Dirty looks at your partner are not permitted. He will enter the point and help you when possible, but remember, he will not intercept low balls angling away from him.

• Be prepared to play *all* balls, as the server must be, and be pleasantly surprised when help is provided.

• Never indulge in "between-point" luxuries of awe and admiration no matter how well you have played your return. Always expect that furry yellow thing to come back one more time.

THE RECEIVER'S PARTNER

Whether or not your team breaks serve is largely dependent on what this player does, or doesn't do, in this court position, just as whether a service game is held depends largely upon what the server's partner does, or doesn't do. The receiver's partner is the dynamic counterpart to the server's partner.

• Protect against the server's partner's poach. Since your eyes are riveted to the server's partner, you will easily see that player begin a poaching move on your partner's return. Move laterally along your service line being careful to stay in line with your opponent's racquet. This movement will often allow you to intercept what would otherwise be a putaway poach. Your first duty in this court position is defense! Take it seriously, and if the server's partner poaches, don't be a coward and bail out. Often a stab at the ball can rescue an otherwise lost point.

• Don't be a linesperson, even if your court position begins on the service line. A good player often lets his receiving partner handle the job of calling the serve in or out so as to watch the potential poacher more carefully. (You call your own service line in singles, don't you?)

• Once you have determined that the

server's partner is *not* making a move to poach your partner's return, immediately assess two factors:

1. Is the server coming to the net behind his serve?
2. What is the height of your partner's return as it crosses the net?

• If the answer to question number one above is no, or if the server is midcourt and the ball *bounces* in front of him, allowing time to choose a shot, question number two above is irrelevant. Immediately claim second volley position. Assume your wall responsibility as the "mirror" of the ball, since the server is perfectly capable of hitting behind you into your alley. (See diagram 26.)

• If the answer to question number one is yes, then question number two becomes very important because the height of the service return to be volleyed by the server determines where you must go next. If the return is high enough to allow the server to volley behind you, into your alley, you must immediately take second volley position and honor the Wall Axiom. (See diagram 27.) This move is critical and yet often neglected by "watchers" and "wonderers" who are sloppy about their court positions. When this court position adjustment is made, it forces the server either to hit crosscourt accurately or pay for allowing his ball to wander toward the person closer to the net—a regrettable "deep to short" error for which you should immediately make him pay. Failure to adjust into second volley position allows the server

to play his shot *anywhere* in the court and be confident that he is hitting "deep to deep."

• If the answer to question number one is yes, and the answer to question number two is "low enough to make the server's first volley difficult," *no matter how wide*, then your wonderful partner has set the stage for you to make one of the most satisfying moves of great doubles. If the server is faced with volleying a low ball off his shoe tops, you know that it will be difficult, if not impossible, for him to change its angle and hit behind you. You are free to move toward the center and be prepared to poach off his weak volley. When you move, you will not know how low his volley will be when it crosses the net. It may even pop over your head. It may even be too wide to reach, but you *do* know that if it is to clear the net at all, it will come back at the same angle your partner created with his splendid return. Now is not the time for hesitation or temerity. Be aggressive! This move is one of the great "one-two punch" combinations in doubles. (See diagram 28.) Your partner hits a great return; you step in and terminate the point with a forcing volley. Never worry about "false moves." Retreat if the ball is too low to make a decent volley. It is possible that the ball might even pop over your head. Remember that your partner is always alert to play *all* balls and will back you up. This move is the counterpart to the server's partner's poach and is as distracting and upsetting to the

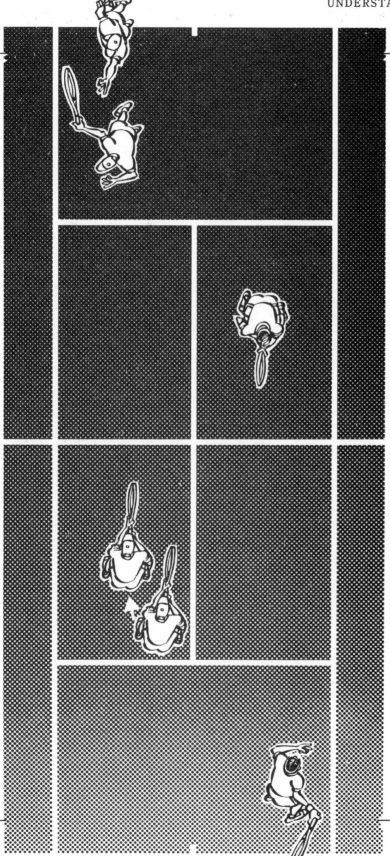

Diagram 26
***When Not to Poach,
Scenario 1***

*The receiver, in the deuce court fore-
ground, has hit an excellent service
return. His partner, in the ad court
foreground, is an excellent volleyer,
renowned for his poaching skills and
is eager to cross and put the ball
away on this point. However, he sees
that the server is not approaching
the net and that his partner's return
will bounce in front of that server.
Since the server can easily aim a
ball into his alley, prudence dictates
that the eager poacher stay home,
honor his wall responsibilities and
wait for a better opportunity.*

Diagram 27
When Not to Poach, Scenario 2

The mad poacher is eager to try again. This time his eyes light up as he sees the server approaching the net, but alas, he suddenly sees that his partner has hit a very ugly return which has cleared the net by a good five feet. If he begins a poach, the server can easily volley into his alley because the ball is so high. Again the patient poacher must cover his alley and await another opportunity.

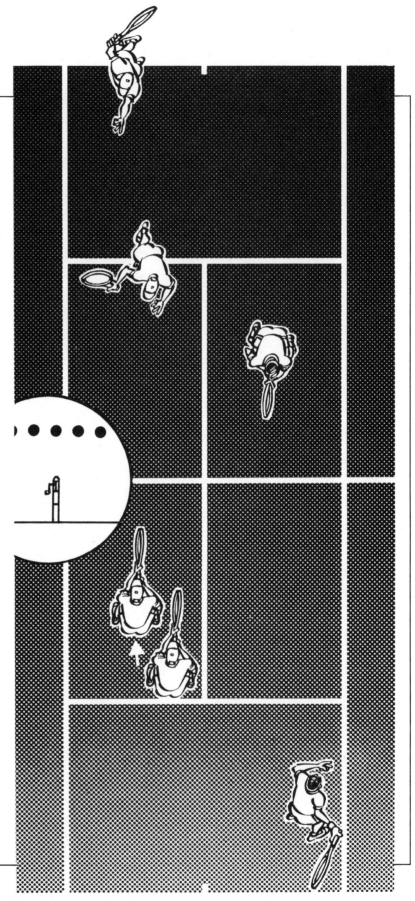

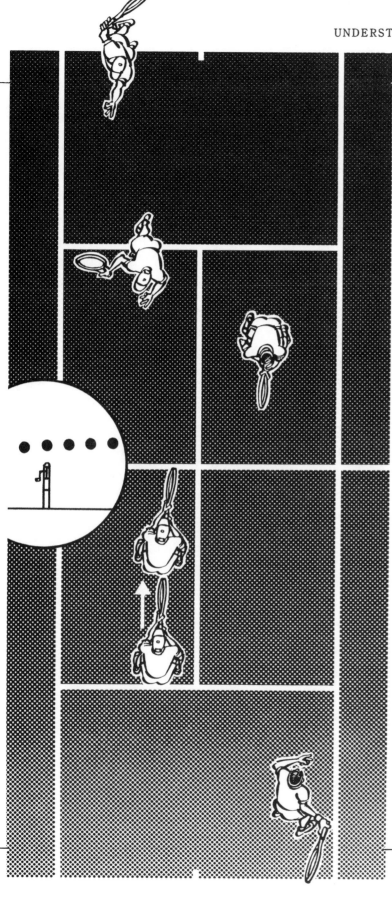

Diagram 28
When to Poach

The passionate poacher is rewarded. His deuce court partner hits a wonderfully low return. The server is approaching the net and will be faced with a volley that he must dig out of his shoetops. It would be virtually impossible for the server to volley this ball into his alley, so the poacher is free to romp across the net, poach what will almost assuredly be a "wounded duck" and terminate the point.

server as the poach is to the receiver. And it is barrels of fun.

Each job on the court is very important, and on each side of the net, proper execution of the "starters'" job—server or receiver—must occur before the "finisher's," servers' and receivers' partners, job may begin. Certainly no job is a place for resting. "Starters" have the responsibility for beginning the point to their team's advantage. "Finishers" have the added pressure of deciding if and when to enter the point, and there is very little time to make that decision. Yet those decisions often determine the outcome of a point, a game or even a match. The ability to play these dynamic "finishing" roles properly and confidently is the culmination of those skills mentioned earlier—covering the center, superior poaching skills, taking care of the lob over your head and knowing your proper court position.

Playing great doubles requires that you see and understand all the tiles in a complicated mosaic. One tile may be beautiful, but meaningless, and yet when each tile is fitted into its proper place, the result is a work of art best viewed by stepping away and appreciating the larger picture.

The great doubles machine functions at a very high level of expertise, which is forged out of each player being in the right place, taking the right ball, saying the right thing, executing jobs well, and playing with a partner you trust and respect.

Jobs Checklist

- ✔ Don't expect to hide or rest in good doubles. Each of the four court positions is a highly visible and demanding job.

- ✔ Your doubles team will achieve its best results when both players enter the majority of the points, achieving a rhythm and balance to the action.

- ✔ Servers and receivers have the responsibility for starting the point to the team's advantage.

- ✔ Service games are often won solely by the aggressive play of the server's partner.

- ✔ Service games are often broken by the dynamic intervention of the receiver's partner into the point.

- ✔ In good doubles, it is particularly true that the whole is greater than the sum of its two parts.

CHAPTER EIGHT

Flexibility: A Powerful Weapon

. . . lucidity of thought . . . freedom from prejudice and from stiffness, openness of mind . . . all these seem to go along with a certain happy flexibility of nature, and to depend upon it.

Mathew Arnold

Imagine playing a match like this one: The score is close, but your team sees the chance to seize some momentum. Suddenly, you are presented with an easy, poachable ball, so you swiftly cross and play the shot to a target, only to watch one of your opponents dive for the ball, close his eyes, recoil, gasp, and hit it off his frame for a clean winner over your and your partner's heads. As you stand there in shocked silence, he apologizes. You think nothing of it until three points later, he does it again. Another apology ensues, this time accompanied by a shoulder shrug. You raise your eyebrows, but your partner tells you not to worry. He can't possibly do it again. You continue to play

your balls to his side of the court whenever possible since he is a gasping, lucky incompetent idiot. Two-and-one-half sets later, not only is he still doing it, but he also manages to win the match on a desperate stab accompanied by a particularly savage groan followed by a sheepish grin. This guy is probably still doing it on somebody else's court to some equally unbelieving opponents.

FLEXIBILITY REQUIRES CONFIDENCE

Stubbornness, hubris and inflexibility are all weaknesses of the "watcher" and "wonderer" teams. The ability to remain flexible in a trying situation such as the one above takes great confidence, both in yourself and

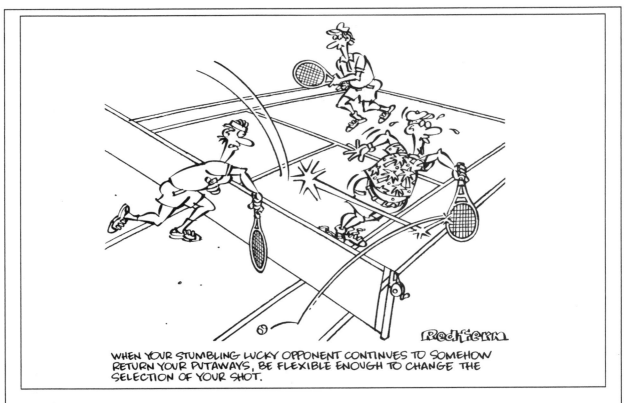

WHEN YOUR STUMBLING LUCKY OPPONENT CONTINUES TO SOMEHOW RETURN YOUR PUTAWAYS, BE FLEXIBLE ENOUGH TO CHANGE THE SELECTION OF YOUR SHOT.

in your partner. When you are winning and things are purring smoothly, flexibility is not a consideration, but it is often the single factor that can rescue your team from a dire situation.

Flexibility, both as a player and as a team, includes the ability to recognize when your strategy is in error, when a different formation or pace shot might produce better results, and when and how to adjust *quickly*. Never wait until you are mired in a mudhole so deep that your adjustments are made only to see if the match can be saved. Learn to evaluate each situation and know your options. Use strategic changes to maintain your lead or stay even in a match, not to try to grasp it from a stinging defeat. Your demon-

stration of flexibility shows your opponents that you have an answer for everything and you will counter every strength they have. The late Arthur Ashe said Jimmy Connors was the greatest player who ever lived because he never lost a match—he just sometimes ran out of time before he could hit upon the winning strategy.

ASK YOURSELF A KEY QUESTION

Being behind in a match is not a personal reflection of how well you are capable of playing tennis, nor is it an indictment on your character. It is frequently a temporary problem for which you can find a solution if you stay flexible and calm, but it can escalate quickly into a hopeless situation if you succumb to blind panic.

Any time the score is not in your favor, regardless of whether you are down one game or six games, the question you and your partner should ask is, "Are they winning or are we losing?" The answer will help you determine which strategy you should use to reverse the tide.

If you are missing manageable volleys, double-faulting, hitting playable balls out or failing to return serve, then they are not *winning*, you are *losing*, and "the fault, dear Brutus, is not in our stars," but on your side of the net. Making winners doesn't win matches, but making unforced errors definitely loses them.

How to Eliminate Unforced Errors

If you determine that the problem *is* the number of unforced errors your team is making, then you must resist the temptation to "hurry and catch up," which will only compound the problem. This is a common pitfall for teams who secretly believe that the people across the net are not really as good as they are. You begin to feel a tinge of embarrassment and hope no one watching realizes that you are down 1-4 to those inferior people across the net. You try to fix it quickly by overplaying balls and trying low-percentage shots, all of which serve to increase the number of unforced errors you make.

If you find yourself down 1-4 and you know that you got there with your own little hatchet, try to be patient. However long it took you to dig yourself into this hole, believe that it will take you twice as long to climb out of it.

HOW TO REGAIN YOUR RHYTHM

Gain composure by playing *longer* points. Resist the temptation to attempt service aces and service return winners. Settle for service returns with too much net clearance, if that is the only way you can get the ball in play. Use more lobs. Take pace off your volleys, even if that means the ball will come back when it shouldn't. The more balls you hit, the more time you will have to settle down and find your rhythm. Give your opponents a chance to make a mistake before you do, and the score should gradually shift in your favor.

What to Do About Forced Errors

If most of the points you are losing are *forced* errors resulting from your opponents' stellar play, then you must change your tactics. Alter your strategy, calmly, and perhaps more than once. The process is frequently one of trial and error; luckily there is no time clock on a tennis court. The following information describes a few tactics.

Sometimes, the better you hit the ball, the better it comes back. Instead of stubbornly trying to hit harder and harder, hoping to knock the racquet out of your opponent's hand, it is more prudent to take pace off of

THE ART OF DOUBLES

your shots, perhaps by using some underspin. If you've ever had an opponent say to you, "Gee, you hit a nice ball," the translation is, "Gee, I love how hard you hit the ball because I never have to do anything but block it." Against those players it is better to hit softly, forcing them to create their *own* pace, which will then elicit, "Gee, I hate to play against junk," which freely translated reads, "You made me work too hard and I don't like it." Make sure you analyze your opponents' ability to handle pace or soft balls and be certain that you are not losing because you are feeding them their preference.

If you and your partner execute favorite shots well, but you don't seem to be winning those points, maybe you are too predictable. Being flexible means acknowledging a tactical flaw such as this without getting angry and trying to hit the shot even *better* or harder. If the guy across the net is standing in the way of your cannonball forehand return and knows it is coming, it is probably a good bet that he's going to get it back, which will only encourage you to hit even harder, perhaps this time finding the fence instead of his racquet. Be flexible and pull a different arrow from your quiver, thus setting the stage for the unexpectedness of your favorite shot.

RECOGNIZE YOUR OWN PREDICTABLE STROKES

One stroke that often becomes much too predictable is the serve. A player with a cannon for a serve may win his service game at love the first time he serves. Then he loses a point or two the next time he serves, and soon wonders why he is losing his serve by the second set. If you allow a good player to see the same ball often enough, he will eventually figure out a way to handle it. Keep receivers off balance by mixing the speed, spin and placement of your serve constantly.

A word of caution: Predictability may be the reason you are losing, but it might also be the reason you are winning. If you have hit the same service return seventeen times in a row, and seventeen times in a row the server has volleyed it into the bottom of the net, don't change it on the off chance that number eighteen *might* come back. Just keep hitting the same old boring winning return.

THE AUSTRALIAN SERVING FORMATION

If you, as the server, have just dumped seventeen straight volleys into the net because that crosscourt service return is too hard to handle, a change in strategy is sixteen muffed volleys overdue. One strategy you should consider using is the Australian serving formation, which is designed to eliminate the receiver's crosscourt return. (See diagram 29.)

To set up this formation, first assume you are serving to the deuce court. Move away from your normal position and stand near the center mark, as if you are playing singles. Your partner, who would normally stand in the ad court facing the deuce court receiver, stands in the *deuce* court and faces the deuce court receiver on the diagonal.

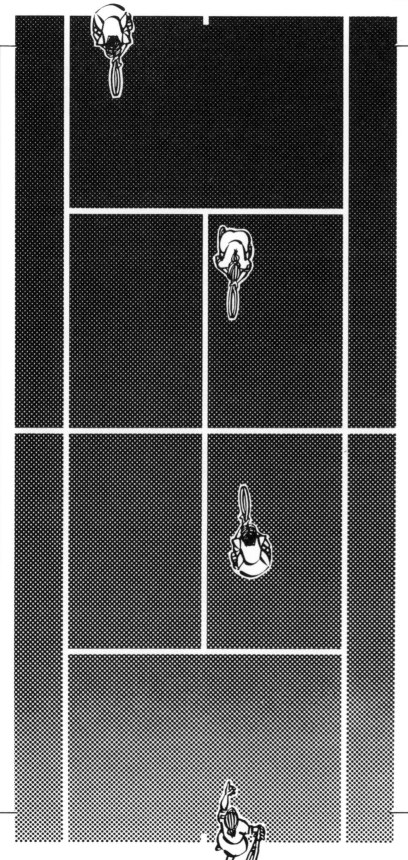

Diagram 29
Using the Australian Serving Formation

The players in the near court are in the Australian serving formation. The server is serving from the base line "T." The partner is positioned in the ad court back far enough in his box to cover a lob and near enough to his alley to prevent a crosscourt service return. The receiver in the far court has adjusted to the server by moving to his left and his partner has repositioned himself very close to the center service line in anticipation of a down-the-line return.

Your partner's exact position is somewhat flexible, but he must stand near enough to the alley to insure that the crosscourt return is no longer possible and far enough away from the net to be able to cover the lob over his head. Many teams serve only down the center when using this formation, but this is not a hard rule. No matter where you serve, if the receiver chooses a "down the line" return rather than a lob, he is faced with the difficult task of changing the direction of the ball toward the higher part of the net. Using the Australian formation frequently forces an otherwise consistent and "grooved" receiver to lose his rhythm and make unforced errors since he must now play his returns in an unfamiliar direction.

Be sure to practice this formation repeatedly before using it in a match. Since the server comes to the net in the "wrong" direction, it may feel "backwards." The server's partner has *total* responsibility for the crosscourt lob because the server's path to the net takes him away from the angle of the ball.

Use this formation when serving either to the deuce or ad court to prevent receivers from hitting devastating crosscourts, or simply use it occasionally to keep the receiving team off-balance. It works well as a surprise tactic in a very long service game when your team needs a quick point.

THE "i" FORMATION

A variation of the Australian formation is the "i" formation, in which your partner positions himself astride the center service line. (See diagram 30.) You, as the server, serve from the center mark and should serve down the middle. Your partner assumes a ready position *below* the level of the net or risks getting hit in the head. Since you begin the point in "i" formation, every point is a signaled poach, with its direction indicated by your partner's hand signal, which you should acknowledge verbally. This formation taxes your partner's endurance and both of your concentrations, but it can effectively confuse the receiving team or lure them into watching the poacher's direction rather than the ball.

DEFENDING AGAINST THE AUSTRALIAN FORMATION

If the Australian formation is used against you, the receiving team, do not let it rattle you. Quickly adjust your thinking and change your targets. Whether you play the deuce court or the ad court, as soon as you see the server move to the center mark, shift slightly away from your alley and toward the center service line to protect against the "down the middle" ace. Your partner should move off the service line and into second volley position, stationing himself as near the center service line as he dare, since you can no longer choose to hit a crosscourt ground stroke.

As receiver, you have only two options: 1) a ground stroke or chipped return down the line that changes the direction of the ball 2) a crosscourt lob over the net player. There

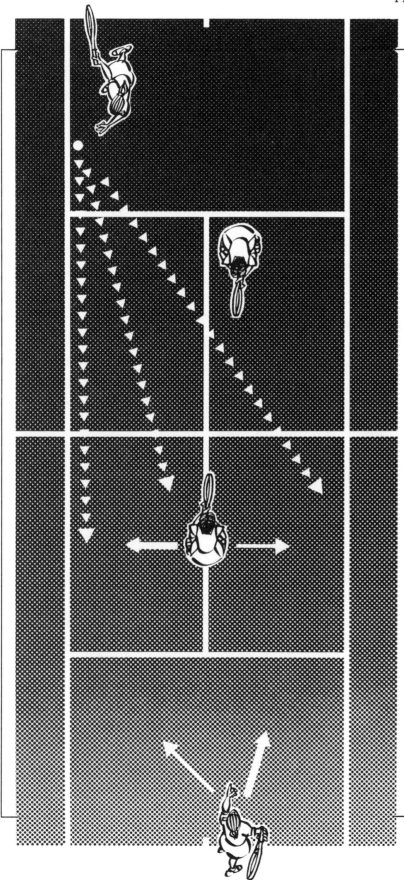

Diagram 30
Using the "i" Serving Formation

The serving team has chosen to use the "i" formation because the team enjoys confusing the opposition with their signaled moves and because the net player crouched in the middle of the court is both agile and an excellent volleyer. Alas, the receiver is a wiley old veteran with many years experience. He has taken two steps backward from his normal receiving position in order to give himself additional time before he must strike the ball. After the serve is struck, the net player and server must begin immediately to move in their signaled directions. The receiver will note the poacher's direction and then aim his return away from him, toward the court to be covered by the server. In this manner, the receiver will always beat the potential poacher at the guessing game. To vary his strategy, this smart receiver may choose to smack a return up the middle, hoping to catch both players going in opposite directions midstride.

are *no* other options; trying to invent one is recklessly foolhardy. (See diagram 31.) If you choose to go down the line with your return, play the ball very early to allow the time you need to get your racquet around and change the direction of the ball.

Your service return will not suffer if you stick to the two "percentage tennis" options described above. Resist the temptation to be a hero and make your opponents *pay for doing this to you*.

DEFENDING AGAINST THE "i" FORMATION

If the "i" formation is used against you, don't panic. Take a few steps back from your normal receiving position to give yourself a little more time. Those extra few seconds will let you see the court and your opponents' movements, especially that of a poaching net opponent who, because of your position adjustment, must now move *before* you hit the ball if he is to cover the court adequately. (See diagram 30.) Once you note the poaching direction, you can safely return the ball back to the server, either crosscourt or down the line, knowing that the ball will be unmolested by the net player. A return played sharply up the middle is often effective against the "i" formation because your opponents are now going in different directions and the ball might land untouched between them. Your partner should not crowd the center against this alignment as he would against Australian or he would block your potential crosscourt. Above all, as with the

Australian, don't allow this different formation to confuse or distract you. Remember your job is to get the ball into play, and that a high, deep lob is never a bad idea.

HOW TO DEFEND AGAINST A MONSTER SERVE

If one of your opponents owns a monster serve that has given both you and your partner fits throughout the match, and you realize that you must break this serve to stay competitive, try beginning each point of the game with both of you in the defensive court position. (See diagram 32.) This does several things. First it gives you more time to return serve because you will play from a stationary position well outside the base line, as if you were playing singles. (Normally, in doubles you would use a service return as an approach shot.) Don't worry that an errant return could drift too close to the net man; your partner's position behind the base line effectively eliminates the opponent's poach. Additionally, the opposing server's rhythm may be thrown off just because the court across the net suddenly looks so different to him. His usual targets are gone, and if you can just get that serve into play he may lose all sense of where to place his first volley. Be careful about your court position and patient enough to approach the net on the proper ball (see chapter three on court position).

You may also use this formation as a serving team, but I don't recommend it, since this relinquishes the advantage your team

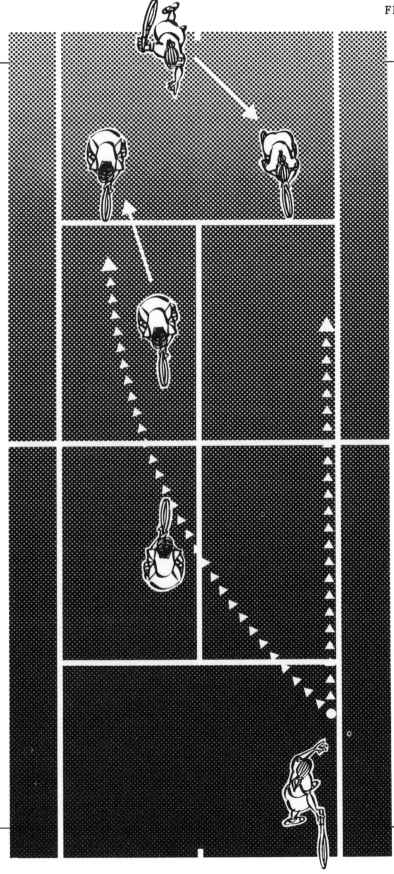

Diagram 31
Defending Against the Australian Formation
When receiving against the Australian formation, return either with a crosscourt lob or a down-the-line chip or drive. No other options exist. Resist the temptation to invent one.

Diagram 32
Returning Serve From the Defensive Court Position
Consider receiving serve from the defensive court position. It gives you the opportunity to take more time with the return, eliminates the worry of a poach and may make your opponents very angry since it indicates to them that much longer points containing a significant number of lobs are on the horizon.

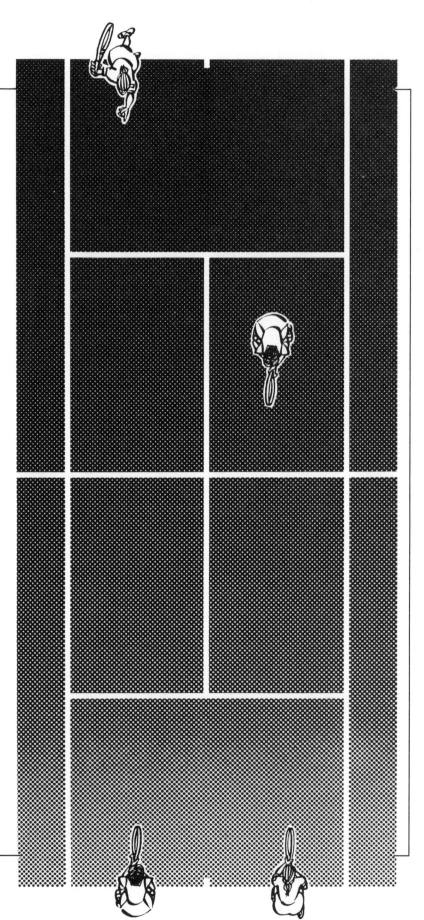

enjoys by starting the point. Any time your team serves, you control the manner in which the point starts, and you do that with the pressure the server's partner puts on the receiver. A poach is always a threat. Good doubles teams maintain the aggressive posture when serving and resort to defense when necessary as the receiving team.

AN EFFECTIVE TACTIC AGAINST IMPENETRABLE OPPONENTS

If the problem is not an opponent's big serve, but simply your inability to make a dent in a good team's otherwise impenetrable armor, the defensive court position formation can be equally effective. Several years ago my partner and I were playing an important match against a fine team that was capable of being either "average" or "brilliant." Unfortunately for us, we met them on a "brilliant" day. We lost the first set 6-0 in what seemed like ten seconds, not because we were making errors, but because they hit winner after winner from impossible places on the court creating angles that I would have thought were simply not options. At 0-6, we, as the receiving team, decided to begin the set from our defensive court position and did so every time they served. This, to our surprise and delight, upset and enraged them so that we won the match 0-6, 6-1, 6-0. Most reversals are not that dramatic, but using good defense can boost you back into a match that would otherwise slip away.

FLEXIBILITY IN THE FACE OF "LOB QUEENS"

If a match is sliding away from you because you are being lobbed to death, there probably isn't a lot you can do except dig in and be patient. So often in this situation one or both players on a team will give in to, "I'm not doing this anymore. This isn't tennis. It isn't fair. If they want it that badly they can have it. I'll go play golf." Then your overheads begin to hit the back fence. The way out of this frustrating dilemma is to relax and appreciate your opponents' strategy. Take it as a compliment. They certainly realize that you volley too well for them to pass you, and so they resort to trying your patience and endurance by hitting every ball twenty feet into the air. No one enjoys having to wrestle with the "lob queens," but you can prevail if you can be flexible. Acknowledge that it will not be over quickly, that you will hit many overheads, that the ball will come back, often, and that this is no time for a temper tantrum. You may win the match 6-2, 6-2, but it may take over two hours. The satisfaction is worth the effort.

IN THE END, BE A GRACIOUS LOSER

If you've tried Australian, used the defensive court position, tried to become less predictable, varied your serves, eliminated your unforced errors and you still cannot prevail, then be satisfied with a job well done. Don't fall victim to hubris, blaming a loss on bad luck. If you've tried everything and nothing worked, maybe your opponents *are* better than you are. Maybe they played over their potential, in the "zone," that day. If so, learn from their performance and have the grace to say, "You played great," not "We played badly." A great doubles team can actually make you play badly if their mastery of the game exceeds yours. It is wise to acquire the capacity to appreciate the artistry.

Flexibility Checklist

- ✔ Ask yourselves, as a team, whether an unfavorable score is due to your own errors or your opponents' superior play. The answer will help you choose the proper strategy to reverse the momentum.

- ✔ Be careful not to become too predictable.

- ✔ Know how to use or defend against the Australian and "i" formations.

- ✔ Never be afraid to offer a good defense to a superior offense.

- ✔ Use strategy changes to help you win matches, not just to prevent you from losing them.

- ✔ If you tried everything and you still lost, it should be a peaceful defeat.

CHAPTER NINE

Achieving Mental Toughness

It is not the critic who counts; . . . the credit belongs to the man who is actually in the arena . . . who at best, knows the triumph of high achievement, and who, at the worst, if he fails, at least fails while daring greatly, so that his place shall never be with those timid souls who knew neither victory nor defeat.

Theodore Roosevelt

Sports psychology is a new and fast developing discipline whose experts have toughened the psyches of tennis players, football teams, baseball pitchers and basketball stars. Masters in the field, such as Dr. James Loehr and Dr. Allen Fox, have published volumes on the importance of relaxation techniques, proper breathing patterns, rituals and positive imaging.

This chapter will not amplify their fine work, but rather analyze some of the peripheral problems that prevent doubles teams from achieving mental toughness. It also discusses some of the strategies that have helped my students and me overcome performance anxiety.

Imagine you and your partner are embroiled in a tough match against gritty opponents. The match has been a real test of wills, but you have managed to break serve at four-all in the third set and you are now serving for the match. Several double faults, weak serves, missed poaches and shaky volleys later, the score is five all, and both you and your partner feel the need for a respirator. What happened?

THE ANGST AND AGONY OF CHOKING

This phenomenon is commonly referred to as "choking," or having an "iron elbow," but what, really, does it mean? When a player chokes a point, he has allowed himself to succumb to what he perceives to be the overwhelming importance of the situation. His breathing becomes irregular, his legs turn to rubber and his muscles, literally, cease to obey the commands from the brain. Fear becomes the overriding emotional state, and the body does not differentiate between fear for one's very life and fear that one cannot serve a tennis ball over the net on this particular point. It senses danger and reacts by constricting blood vessels and muscles and going to a red alert. It is no wonder that a server choking before a match point can't get the service toss to leave his hand, or if it does, it flies ten feet behind him. In this psychological state, a smooth service toss is impossible. The muscles simply can't obey.

Every player chokes points, and you and your partner should acknowledge this, dismiss those points as part of the natural flow of the match, and get on with the business of winning. If, however, your team chokes games, sets or matches, then you are not capable of turning those important and stressful situations into challenges to play your best tennis. You should evaluate the psychological health of your team, searching for patterns of choking or circumstances that create losing syndromes.

That server who frittered away a chance to win the match at 5-4 in the third set with a pitiful display of double faults and shaky volleys was probably secretly saying to himself, "Please, God, let them make four mistakes in a row and it will be over." What in fact befell this server, and no doubt his partner too, was an anxiety attack that made them stop playing to win, and instead start playing simply not to lose. This primarily occurs when a team is ahead, not behind, in the score. At 4-4, or even 4-5, your team is still embroiled in the battle and focused on your "jobs on the court." Your only burden is staying in the match, an onus much easier to bear than the responsibility for winning the match, which you would carry if you were ahead 5-4. When your team is one game away from victory, it is incumbent upon you to actively *win* the match—to continue to take risks under the pressure of needing to close out the match. Great doubles teams are experts at this, but inexperienced teams who have played a brilliant match up to this point will often fall victim to "trying not to lose" and will fail to deliver that masterful, aggressive performance at this crucial juncture where it is most needed.

CONQUERING THE TWO GREATEST FEARS ON COURT

Fear of losing and fear of winning are different maladies born of other causes. They go together and are often present even before the match begins.

Fear of losing is a much more common problem when you play a team you or others feel you should beat. Often, before you ever take the court, devilish thoughts are bouncing off the walls of your psyche:

"Oh, my God, what will people say if we lose to *these guys*?"

"I won't be able to explain it if they even take a set from us."

"If we lose this one, the world will collapse into raucous and hysterical laughter and I will be forced to kill myself."

Already, before the first ball has been struck in the warm-up, the seeds of self-destruction are in place and optimum performance may be a goal for your Shetland Sheepdog but not for you on this day. Once this downward spiral begins, it is very difficult to reverse. Lack of confidence breeds fear of losing, which triggers fear of embarrassing yourselves, which puts two monster egos on the court instead of two tennis players, which makes losing the match a distinct possibility. All of which combine to create that sick feeling in the pit of your stomach that whispers the simple truth: "This ranks right up there with having a root canal and I *really* don't want to be here."

The following are strategies for overcoming performance anxiety.

PLAY THE BALL, NOT THE PEOPLE

The first thing you and your partner should do to avoid this self-destructive spiral is to leave your egos at home and convince yourselves that all opponents are worthy of your complete respect, even if you find they don't even know how to keep score. Never compare your expertise with that across the net. Ignore it and remember that you are playing the *ball*, not people. The ball may come off your opponents' racquets in a most disconcerting manner, but your challenge is to respond to those oddities, not to blame the people for hitting balls in an unorthodox style.

GET CENTERED IN THE "NOW"

Once the match has started, get out of your head and into the match, and stay there. All good sports psychologists agree that in order to give an optimum performance it is vital that you stay centered in the "now." There are many excellent training methods for achieving that state. Some of the best techniques are described in *Mental Toughness Training* by Robert Tutko of San Jose State University. Choose one that enables you to rid yourself of past ("I can't believe how poorly I played that last point") and future ("How can I win my serve next time?") concerns. Concentrate fully on the next point and nothing else.

FOCUS ON YOUR COURT JOB

When the match gets tight, stay positive and confident with your shoulders back, posture erect, and concentrate only on your "job on the court." Stay determined to execute your responsibility in each court position without worrying about the consequences of mistakes. If you remain calm and focused, and doggedly discharge your duties as you know them, the match will play itself, and the outcome will take care of itself. It takes many hours of match play before a team can finally grasp that if you have the confidence to hit your shots against inferior opponents, you will win, and if you allow fear to keep you from executing properly, you most definitely will lose. It's your choice.

CONQUER YOUR FEAR OF WINNING

When you find that you are playing "up," with nothing to lose against the team seeded number one, things are much easier, until you wake up and realize you are winning. One of the greatest sources of fun a team can have in a match, with the possible exception of playing "in the zone" and pulverizing your opponents, is playing in a situation where you are not expected to win, and playing well enough to scare the opposition, but never being in any danger of winning. This is the classic "no pressure because we've got nothing to lose" scenario in which you and your partner probably play some of your very best tennis.

All is well until this "very best tennis" is suddenly good enough to make the match very close. Then, alas, the fear of winning, fear of being successful against all odds, rears its ugly head. The symptoms are exactly like those of "fear of losing" but the small, destructive voices are singing different tunes:

"Hey—they were ranked #1 last year and we're up 4-1 in the first set. Oh, my God . . ."

"Gee, this isn't so hard. Maybe we're really as good as they are? No way . . ."

"What are they waiting for? Surely they have some secret weapon we haven't seen yet . . ."

"If we win this . . . if we beat them . . . if we really win this . . . if we win . . . oh, but we couldn't possibly beat them . . ."

Unlike fear of losing, fear of winning generally sets in after a match has begun. In this case, stellar play begins to deteriorate when the possibility of winning becomes feasible. The downward spiral begins with faltering confidence in the face of unexpected success, leading to tentative shot making, which allows the "favored" team back in the match, which permits you both to believe that winning one set was more than you had hoped for anyway. This attitude, ultimately, insures the expected loss of the match and explains why the scores of underdog teams against seeded teams are often losses of 7-5, 6-1, or 7-6, 6-0, or even 4-6, 6-1, 6-0. Here are four ways to prevent fear of winning:

1. Build up a generous measure of confidence bordering on cockiness in order to offset your team's and others' lopsided expectations for the outcome. Fear of success is a very real psychological phenomenon experienced by any doubles team on the court battling not only theoretically superior opponents, but also that team's confidence and reputation.

2. Imagine the match as the opportunity you have worked for and rightfully earned. Do not be content with think-

ing that at least you have made a good showing and made it into a close match. Welcome the chance to prove your worth. Do not shrink from it.

3. Stick with your "job on the court," recognizing that a potential upset situation may elicit an even better performance from a worthy opponent.

4. Embrace the chance to turn your game up a notch to keep pace with determined foes. You may not win this kind of a match the first time you try, but you will sleep well knowing that you battled toe to toe with a favored team, rather than admit that you folded your tent early and mentally tiptoed off the court in defeat before the last point was over.

SEIZE THE DAY

When you and your partner are pitted against a team of equal ability and the outcome of the match is seen as a toss-up, you must not only be mentally tough, but you must also be eagerly searching for ways to seize the momentum of the match.

"Watchers" and "wonderers" tend to ignore the importance of momentum and often attribute close wins to luck and close losses to "that one net-cord that fell your way." On the other hand, one of my league teams, "The Competitors," feels that momentum is such an important dimension they have emblazoned *carpe diem* as a team motto on their sweatshirts. Making things happen in a tight match really depends on your team's ability to "seize the day."

In a contest between two even teams, it is unrealistic to expect to grasp the momentum early in the first set and keep it until the conclusion of the match. The tug of war for psychological control continues well into the second or third set, the balance often shifting in favor of one team or another as many as four or five times. In the end, the team that capitalizes on the opportunity to win many points in a row, without making unnecessary errors that negate their advantage, will prevail.

So many times a team will break serve by waging a monumental battle only to drop their own service game without winning a point. If you are to seize momentum in a match, you must recognize a service break as an opportunity to punish your opponents psychologically. Do everything you can not to relax mentally in a situation that demands added care and concentration.

If you have just won an exhausting service game after being down 0-40, you have some degree of momentum at this stage of the match, particularly since your opponents are probably kicking themselves for having let that game get away. Don't let them regain the control they have just given you. You will be tempted to heave a sigh of relief and relax after the tension of the previous game. It only takes you and your partner missing two service returns and your opponents getting a let-cord winner to arrive at 40-0; the match is now psychologically even again.

GO FOR THE JUGULAR

If you are to be truly mentally tough and eager to seize the momentum of a match, anytime you detect a chink in the armor you must go for the jugular. Here are four ways to do just that:

1. When the net man misses a poach off your partner's return, hit your next return right at him—not to cause bodily injury but because he might be so concerned with his previous error that he will miss again.
2. If you detect that an opponent is feeling shaky about his serve, stand near the service line when you receive in order to let him know his nervousness is no secret.
3. Whenever you are the lucky recipient of a let-cord winner, try hard not to even the score by losing the next point carelessly.
4. If you see that an opponent lacks confidence, play most of your shots in his direction whenever possible.

These tactics are not immoral or unethical in any way. They are strategies for exercising psychological superiority over your opponents, and thus over the match. If it is true that 65 percent of tennis is mental, as has often been said, then your ability to dominate psychologically and ultimately seize and retain the momentum of a match is much more important than your stroke production.

REMEMBER THESE FINAL WISDOMS

To be mentally tough, your team must display increasing grace and courage as a situation becomes more difficult. No matter how dire the outlook, keep your perspective and be gentle with yourself and your partner. If you are struggling against tough opponents and are fighting yourself or your partner, your team is severely outnumbered. You have enough problems across the net without creating unnecessary obstacles on your own side.

Constant self-criticism or criticism of your partner, although it may be unspoken, is an indication that you are measuring your performance against some mythical standard of play that you have set. Learn to play with the weapons you have brought to the court; don't pine for those you left at home. Freeing yourself that day from self-concept removes limitations, so if you didn't manage to bring a blockbuster first serve to the court, it is far more constructive to embrace the capabilities of your second serve than to spend the match berating yourself for not owning something that simply does not belong to you that day. It doesn't mean you *can't* serve. It means that for whatever reason, you must serve *differently* in that match. If you can't hit a forehand drive on a given day, stop trying. Chip the ball instead. Search your quiver for a different arrow to sling rather than railing against fate for crippling your arsenal.

PRACTICE BEING TOUGH

Being a mentally tough competitor takes constant practice. It is not a skill like riding a bicycle—learned once and then possessed forever. The expression "match tough" is an important one. It refers to the number of times you have competed under pressure and experienced "closing a match out," coming from behind to win, winning the close one, or winning when it is not expected of you. While you can practice your volleys by drilling in a relaxed atmosphere, mental toughness is the one part of your game that can only be practiced under pressure. In addition, if you don't play pressure-filled matches, your toughness will evaporate. To give a truly tough performance, you not only must have the courage to hit your best shots under pressure, but you must also have practiced those shots enough to ensure a reasonable chance that they will stay in the court when you most need them to—during the big points.

The year Arthur Ashe won Wimbledon, a reporter found him out on a practice court an hour before the finals of the tournament practicing his serve. It was an unusually warm day in England and the reporter watched as Ashe served perhaps one hundred balls, all of which hit some part of a service line. Having served what appeared to be one hundred aces, Ashe picked up all of the balls and proceeded to repeat the entire process. The reporter could stand it no longer and asked him why, if he had just hit every line in the service court, would he want to practice serving another hundred balls in the heat just before a Wimbledon final. Ashe replied, "So that I can hit *one* under pressure."

DISPLAY A WINNING ATTITUDE

Mentally tough teams display a winning attitude from the very first point, and it does not go unnoticed by the opposition. Mentally fragile teams convey a willingness to lose without a fight and it shows. If you think back to the last few matches you played, you can probably point to teams you have encountered who displayed characteristics typical of tough competitors as well as some that you just knew had no will to win.

Remember, in order to acquire the character of a team that is psychologically tenacious and unwilling to beat themselves, you must learn that an ugly "W" is *always* better than a pretty "L." Stand out there as long as it takes and do whatever it takes to win. You don't earn national ranking with pretty strokes.

Winning is definitely more fun than losing, but failure is a necessary part of the learning experience. If you try to learn just one thing every time you lose a match, you can make those losses into stepping-stones that lead to a more solid performance in the future, and yet, there will always be unexplainable "bad losses." It is an irony of the game that absolute mental toughness and a demeanor impenetrable to the emotional strain of match play is always a goal just out of reach. Achieving mental toughness is a process that is never finished. It is a constantly illusive dream that you grasp by the fingers. Sometimes you hold on. Sometimes you don't. Meanwhile, insecurity and lack of confidence will always nip at your heels.

PLAY TO *WIN*

Mentally tough teams always play to win. They never play to avoid losing. Above all, they have learned to keep their perspective. They have learned that there are great days, so-so days, and days when racquet-smashing seems like a better sport.

The next time your team is embroiled in a tense match where points have been choked away and fear of losing or fear of winning is starting its ugly chant, stop. Stop everything and discuss with your partner how the loss of this one match will seriously, irrevocably, and forever diminish your lives as tennis players, as citizens, as bird-watchers, as PTA members, or as human beings. The answer should make you both relax—and smile.

Mental Toughness Checklist

- ✔ Everybody chokes points, but if you choke games or matches, take stock of your team's psychological health.

- ✔ Never succumb to the "trying not to lose" syndrome. No matter what the score, force things to happen.

- ✔ Remember that fear of losing can seriously compromise your ability to perform even the easiest tasks under pressure.

- ✔ Remember that fear of winning will cost you the upset win you "almost had" but let get away.

- ✔ To become mentally tough, stop the destructive voices in your head and stick to your "jobs on the court."

- ✔ Wrest the momentum from tough opponents and learn to seize the day.

- ✔ The impenetrable armor of unflappable absolute confidence at all times is a myth. Mental toughness is a constant struggle needing eternal practice and patience.

CHAPTER TEN

Gaining Command of the Intangibles

"Mr. Kikady, how do you maintain your concentration,
stay relaxed and maintain accuracy under the pressure
of playing for hundreds of thousands of dollars?"
"I do not know, but I think, it is not by strength but by art."

Sandy Dunlop

Great doubles teams make a series of complicated actions look deceptively easy and graceful. Denise McCluggage, writing in *The Centered Skier*, says, "Grace is a warmer word for efficiency." Four centuries ago, the Italian diplomat Baldassare Castiglione introduced the word *sprezzatura* in *The Book of the Courtier*. The English language does not possess a word that conveys all that is meant by this Italian term. It refers to a certain casualness, a grace of movement, even a kind of natural, off-handed manner which, while giving the impression of absolute effortlessness, is actually acquired through tedious hours of practice and strict discipline. Castiglione says further of those who possess *sprezzatura:*

For it implants in the minds of the spectators the notion that one who so easily does well knows how to do much more than what he is doing, and if he expended study and labor on what he is doing he could do it much better . . . Likewise, in dancing a single step, a solitary graceful and effortless movement of the body quickly reveals the proficiency of the dancer.

When you watch great doubles teammates perform their jobs correctly, you marvel at the ease with which a perfectly placed service return is executed off a very difficult serve. You stare in admiration as the receiver's partner crosses in front of his teammate at precisely the right moment to end the point with his poach. Not only is the skill readily apparent from the actions of the players, but the sense that there are reserves of ability, as yet undisplayed, is also present. Nothing looks difficult or awkward. Although it is true that the whole is most definitely greater than the sum of its parts, when analyzing what makes a superior doubles team, certain "intangibles" are common to all of them.

TIME: THERE NEVER SEEMS TO BE ENOUGH

One of the most frequent complaints I hear from aspiring doubles stars is that there simply isn't enough time to hit a shot correctly and accurately. Therefore, their most frequent error is that they rush every movement, every stroke, every ball they hit. It is not uncommon for inexperienced players to serve, race toward the net as fast as they can run and swing wildly at the ball somewhere along the route in this frantic sprint toward total disaster. They are propelled at full gallop by the absolute conviction that all balls travel at speeds in excess of 200 miles per hour.

By contrast, great players always seem to be in slow motion, never rushed, never hurried, never flustered, for two very good reasons.

Reason 1:

In order to become a master of time you must develop proper ball-watching skills, but it is simply not true that you should *always* watch the ball.

Poor doubles players will turn around and watch their partners hit the ball, hoping that this will provide some clue as to what might happen next. Although average players know better than that, *they* will focus on the ball as it crosses the net going *toward* the opponents in order to perceive its direction. In addition, both poor and average players watch the ball come off their own strings and follow it with their eyes until it lands across the net, and often longer. Highly skilled players, on the other hand, understand that you must always track the ball as it is coming *toward* you, but *never* watch the ball as it is going *away* from you.

Imagine you are the player striking the ball. You know where you intend to hit it, so you know beforehand which opponent will strike the ball next. The moment the ball leaves your strings, your eyes should move to that player's racquet, never pausing for an instant to follow the flight of your shot. Realize that the ball and your opponent's racquet are going to end up in the same place at the same time.

If your partner is the one striking the ball, you will not know its direction so readily. In this case, resist the temptation to peek at the ball and discipline yourself to have, to use John Madden's expression, "linebacker eyes." This means that while the ball is on your partner's strings, your eyes should be darting from opponent to opponent and back until you see one of their racquets begin its preparation. That player becomes your opponent and it is his racquet that you must read and react to.

Proper ball-watching skills will allow you to act on your volleys instead of reacting to the ball at the last second. Good eye control will give you at least two to three more seconds to see what you must do to prepare properly to play your shot and will help you to realize that you need not rush all of your strokes. Again, only watch the ball when it is coming toward you—never when it is traveling away from you.

Reason 2:

Highly skilled players have the confidence to take the time they need to execute the shot properly. There is absolutely no substitute for early preparation, but, as I endlessly try to convince my students, there is always more time than you think. The trick is to discipline yourself to understand the natural rhythm of a stroke, that is, the cadence of a free-flowing weight transfer and swing of the racquet and to know through practice the amount of time necessary to execute it smoothly, and to have the confidence that the required amount of time exists for the taking. In *The Sweet Spot in Time*, John Jerome says:

Most infield errors occur because the fielder starts his play before he catches the ball. A lot of dropped forward passes fall to the turf because the receiver starts avoiding tacklers before he finishes catching the football. This is the tiredest cliché in sports, of course—"Look the ball into your hands," even "Keep your eye on the ball"—but it illuminates a little more territory when it is understood in terms of available time. The good performer simply takes all the time there is for the particular move.

Great doubles teams are composed of players who do not watch each other hit the ball, but instead keep their eyes focused on opponents' racquets. They will find a way, even in the most heated exchanges at the net, to use every available second to hit a controlled and accurate shot. The issue of time is a very important one in tennis. If you have enough of it, it is your team's greatest ally, and if you give your opponents too much of it, they will always find ways to pick you apart.

Therefore, you must find ways to create more time for your team and take it away from the opposing team. You must give a fluid, graceful, unhurried and relaxed performance while compelling your opponents to look harried, rushed and unable to think clearly. Your ability to do so is predicated on your understanding of superior racquet work.

YOUR OPPONENTS HAVE CALLED 911 AND NEED RESPIRATORS; DON'T IMPRESS THE CROWD WITH A SMOKING VOLLEY TO THE BASELINE. GET THE BALL IN AND WIN THE POINT!

WHEN TO USE DEPTH, PACE OR FINESSE

Have you ever watched a doubles team work a point until one opponent is off the court and the other lies prone in an alley, only to blow the easy volley into the middle of the back fence? It happens often and is the result of not choosing the racquet speed sufficient to accomplish the task at hand. Overkill, hitting a ball much too hard when placement to open court is sufficient, and underkill, failure to use pace to push a volley past a well-positioned opponent, are maladies of the inexperienced players.

Three intangibles great doubles teams have mastered are knowing when to volley with pace, when to place a volley deep in the court and when to use finesse. *Pace* is a function of the speed of the racquethead through a volley and of an ability to bring the racquet to a sudden stop. It is used in what is commonly referred to as the "punch volley." *Depth* is a function of the distance the racquet travels from contact point forward, that is, the length of the follow-through. *Finesse* is the ability to create "touch volleys" by softening the grip on the racquet and "coddling" the ball to create a soft, short volley that carries underspin. If you are to become an expert in choosing the appropriate racquet speed for the job, you must understand these guidelines:

• Pace is achieved with "short and quick" racquet work.

• Depth is achieved with "long and slow" racquet work.

• Finesse is achieved by caressing the ball with a gentle hand.

• Hitting for both depth and pace will almost always send your ball over the base line (or the sideline) and out.

• Using a short but slow racquet speed will either send the ball into the bottom of the net or give an opponent much too much time to choose his weapon.

• Use "long and slow" to take away the timing space of an opponent parked near the base line.

• Reserve "short and quick" for those times when the pace on your ball must keep an opponent who is in a "short" court position from having the time to react to your shot.

• Remember that the primary target on the court is always the ground in front of your opponent. Use "long and slow" for "deep to deep" volleys and "short and quick" for "short to short" volleys. Stick with this formula and your opponents will never have enough time to pick a shot that can hurt you. (See diagram 33.)

Cultivate the Drop or Underspin Volley

There is nothing more frustrating than seeing your opponents hugging the base line and not being able to play the ball gently enough to have it drop unplayed in front of them.

The solution is to cultivate the drop volley or softly angled underspin volley. These volleys can also create more time for you and your teammate to reposition yourselves in an emergency. If, for example, you are pulled very wide on a volley and you hit it back with a great deal of pace, you may not have the time to recover your court position before your opponent strikes the ball. However, if you play the ball softly, or finesse the shot back over the net with underspin, you will give yourself time to prepare for the next ball.

Hitting with finesse is not easy. It requires a "soft" hand on the racquet—a looser grip—and the technique is made more difficult to master with the new wide-body racquets. These racquets are extremely powerful (and can add many miles per hour to your strokes), but they make learning to take pace off a ball quite a challenge. Nevertheless, it is an art worth mastering both because it can create precious time for you and your partner and because finesse is always the "fake 'em out of their Nikes" element of surprise guaranteed to wrong-foot even the most skillful foe.

In general, never be too ambitious for the situation at hand. Many times a moderate and controlled racquet speed will do the job. Experienced players resist the temptation to be a hero on every volley, choosing instead to win the point with an unglamorous but effective placement into the open court. Fence-bashers believe that bone-crushing

Diagram 33
Racquet-Speed Guidelines

The player in the near deuce court is demonstrating the following guidelines:

A. A short follow-through and slow racquet speed is insufficient for a ball to clear the net.

B. Use a long follow-through and slow racquet speed to send a ball deep to the shoes of a base-line hugger.

C. Trying to hit for both depth and pace, using a long follow-through and fast racquet speed, will send the ball over the base line.

D. Use a short follow-through and quick racquet speed to punish a ball in the "short to short" direction and thus end the point.

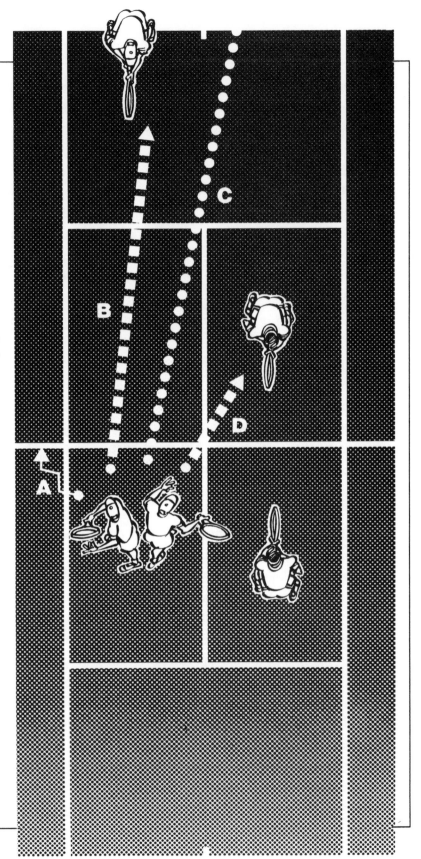

pace is beautiful. Successful doubles teams know that discretion is always the better part of true heroism on the court. There are no points for style in tennis.

ANTICIPATION MEANS NO MORE SCRAMBLING

Skilled teams never look rushed, for two reasons: 1) the time they make available to themselves, and 2) their racquet-reading skills permit them to move in an indicated direction before the opponent has completed his shot. The lack of last-minute, frantic scrambling to reach a ball is commonly referred to as "anticipation." Players who are said to have great anticipation are not lucky guessers, but rather astute racquet-watchers who have learned to glean enough information from what they see to glide into position before the ball actually arrives. Good anticipation gives a team the luxury of taking all available time to execute a shot and remain unflustered.

On page 5 Jack Kramer was quoted as wishing that his "dream" doubles partner possessed a "feel" for anticipation, and he suggested that the skill has four components:

1. Placement of your own shot.
2. Knowledge of the types of strokes an opponent prefers.
3. Concentration on the opponent's motions as he is striking the ball.
4. Shifting position to meet the return.

Placement of Your Own Shot

By understanding the geometry of the court you can place shots that let you position your team for the returns your opponent has the *highest* probability of executing. Meanwhile you should ignore your opponents' return options that have the lowest chance of success.

Court geometry means that angles beget angles. For example, balls hit up the middle will generally come back down the middle. The first step in learning to anticipate an opponent's return is to know and play for what nine out of ten players will hit. For example, when out of position, a player will lob. When presented with options, a player will generally try to drive the ball, usually up the middle, since "pound the middle" has been the doubles mantra for years. When presented with the opportunity to hit a sharply angled volley because a player is standing in his own alley, he will almost always take it.

A word of caution: The concept of *time* is again of crucial importance. If you take away an opponent's timing space, his ball will have to rise if it is to clear the net. If that player is positioned on the base line, his ball *will* be a lob; if positioned at the net, his ball *will* be one you can close on and put away. Know this, move before the ball is struck, and you will have *anticipated* the response. If, however, you give an opponent all the time he needs to choose any one of many possible responses, none of the above is viable and your team is simply helpless, or to use the vernacular, "you guys are dead meat."

Know Your Opponent's Preferred Strokes

Knowing an opponent's stroking preference is easy if you meet him in every tournament. The idiosyncrasies, preferences and habits of a first-time opponent may take you a set to master but be patient. You will see that almost all players have a pattern of shots they use in sequence or they have a "pet" shot. Once you see a response in a particular tactical situation, play for that shot in every similar situation. Never think "surely he'll do something different this time" until you *see* something different. Players believe in their idiosyncrasies passionately and are reluctant to change them. A player who loves his "down the line" service return will continue to hit it even if you are standing in the alley, because he believes in his shot more than he believes in your ability to cover it adequately.

Concentrate on Your Opponent's Motions

Concentration on an opponent's ball-striking motion is predicated on your ability to watch his racquet diligently and relentlessly. If he is about to hit a ground stroke, you must observe not only his racquet preparation but also his foot placement and shoulder turn. If he is about to volley, you need *only* watch the racquet because racquet angle determines where the volley goes, regardless of whether a player is aiming a ball intentionally or simply reacting accidentally.

Kramer states that "these details may appear to be complicated, but after practice they can be noted at a glance." In my experience, I would say that inexperienced students have a great deal of trouble mastering this skill. Most worry that they are unable to fathom some mysterious, transcendental revelation that racquet-watching communicates to the rest of the world. But after many court hours, you will be able to see the adjustments in your opponent's physical stance and see the ball come off a racquet at a certain angle. You will find that you have ample time to prepare to hit the ball. It isn't that *watching* the racquet gives you a magical head start, but that *not* watching it will give you no time to prepare your racquet or adjust your court position.

Shift Position to Meet the Return

Finally, strict attention to your team's wall responsibilities (see chapter three) will insure that all high-percentage strokes aimed at you will never land unplayed on your side of the net. Remember to stay positioned in the *middle* of the probable angles of return. Do not position yourself to defend against the opponent's difficult-to-execute, low-percentage shot. If your team is positioned to intercept what you perceive to be your opponent's most likely responses and to concede the most difficult shots on the court, you will win the match.

Anticipation takes time to develop. There is no time to study probabilities and assess options in the heat of battle; thus trial and error is the only learning method. Determination and a great deal of patience will ultimately pay great dividends.

TWO RULES OF PROPER COURT MOVEMENT

All great doubles players look as if they are gliding around the court on ice skates. This impression comes from their ability to keep their bodies over their feet and to change directions effortlessly.

Rule 1: Incorporate a Check-Step

The first rule of proper movement on the court is that you must incorporate a "check-step" (also called a "split-step," "split-stop," or, as one of my students said, "a pause for no more than a heartbeat") into your game. A check-step is when you stop your feet and bring them together every time an opponent strikes a ball. It lets you move in any one of four directions—forward, left, right or backward—and react to your opponent's ball in a balanced and controlled manner. Failure to make a check-step is the main reason inexperienced players lunge at balls and find themselves flailing when they should be choosing appropriate responses. For all good players, this momentary pause is absolutely automatic and is never omitted. Unless you are serving, all good doubles players execute the check-step upon hearing the opponent's racquet strike the ball. However, if you are serving, "check" when your ball *lands* in the service box. In theory, this is the only time in a doubles point that the ball will *bounce*, and "checking" earlier will allow you more time

to adjust direction or rate of speed toward the net on a particularly wide or low return of service. With this exception, all good doubles players "split" on the sound of the ball every single time it is struck by an opponent. This means that if you are the server's partner, there may be a service return and perhaps two or three volleys aimed at your partner. While you have not played a single ball, you will have made three or four check-steps. You can never afford to be moving when your opponent is striking a ball because the odds of being "wrong-footed" on the shot are simply too great. Checking on impact across the net will allow you to move in any direction with grace and balance.

Rule 2: Always Move to and Through Each Shot

The other component to the "ice-skating" effect created by good players is that they are always moving forward. To become a great doubles player you must learn to not only move *to* a ball but also *through* it. To emulate these players, learn to return serve while moving forward and to hit your first volley while moving toward the net. (Remember: All approach shots to the net are hit while moving forward, and in doubles, both your service return and your first volley are technically approach shots.) This is not license to run through all of your shots, but in order to be effective, you must give up the "stop, turn, step, hit" mentality.

To maintain your balance while moving

through these shots, to be an iceskater and not a leaning-over lunger who "squats and swats," practice setting your weight on your pivot foot at the very instant you strike the ball. For instance, if you are a right-handed player hitting a backhand service return or first volley, gather your weight on your left leg just as the racquet meets the ball, and then immediately continue forward onto your right leg.

Split-steps, movement forward (in a balanced and controlled fashion at an appropriate rate of speed), agility (not foot speed), and proper use of the pivot foot all combine to give the great doubles player the look of a graceful skater.

THE GIFT OF GREAT HANDS

One of the things said consistently of the greatest doubles players is that they have "great hands." Unfortunately, I do not believe this ability can be taught. That is not to say that you cannot be a master of the game of doubles without this gift, but it is a wonderful asset if you have it. Players with great hands seem to have a knack for reflexing balls that would otherwise be putaways back across the net. They display great courage and concentration in situations that would have less bold players bailing out and running for the sidelines. They have either 1) more highly developed racquet-watching skills and so superior knowledge of where the opponent will likely try to put the ball, 2) great luck, 3) tremendous "feel" and instinct for net-play, or 4)

all of the above. In any event, if you are lucky enough to have a player of this caliber for a partner, make sure you buy him a birthday present. His skill is worth several points a game.

THE SUM OF THE PARTS

A great doubles team's easy grace, air of confidence and appearance of great reserves of ability are the result not just of many practice hours, but of actual time on the court gaining match experience. There are no shortcuts to mastery. If it were possible to take two human beings and teach them every skill needed to execute every shot perfectly on the doubles court, they would be technically perfect, yet unable to beat anybody. To achieve mastery, your team must gain, through time, its own character and style, intangibles that are direct results of the number of hours, days and years you have played the game. *Sprezzatura* develops slowly and cannot be purchased at any price.

The seasoned, experienced and successful doubles team expresses wholeness and harmony in its artistic execution of movements that in less-skilled teams look awkward and clumsy.

Efficiency of movement, the confidence to take your time, proper balance and a low center of gravity while moving forward, good anticipation and the gift of "great hands" are intangibles that will give your doubles team the look of mastery, and the visage of winners who will strike fear and terror in the hearts of your opponents.

Mastering the art of doubles takes time, patience and dogged determination. The skills develop slowly, improving at times by entire levels, and at others by only inches. The struggle is worth it, I think, because it will make your results so much more rewarding. More importantly, I believe the process will teach you to love the game passionately. The best thing to give to an endeavor is your love, and next, your labor. When you can combine them the product is indeed a very rich experience.

Recently, I had the privilege of meeting Louise Brough, Wimbledon doubles champion and U.S. Open champion with Margaret Osborne DuPont from 1942-1950 and from 1955-1958. Her humility and graciousness were charming. But when I asked her which of all of her titles meant the most to her, she replied, "All of them, my dear. Every single one."

Intangibles Checklist

✔ Acquire the graceful efficiency of a great doubles team, *sprezzatura*, through strict discipline and mastery of certain "intangibles."

✔ Develop your racquet-watching skills in order to anticipate opponent's shot and gain time for your own. Use all available time to hit your shots.

✔ Master depth, pace and finesse to keep from over- or underplaying your own shots and to rob the opposition of the time they need to execute shots properly.

✔ Know that developing good anticipation is a necessity and is learned slowly, and painfully, through experience.

✔ Master the "check-step" and force yourself to keep pressure on your opponents by relentlessly moving forward.

✔ Don't hurry the process of becoming a great doubles team. You cannot play masterful matches before it is time.

CHAPTER ELEVEN

Drills for Honing Your Skills

Practice is the best of all instructors.

Publilius Syrus

By practicing only a little bit, or with-out enthusiasm, you can gradually let the task of improving overwhelm you. It is a misconception to believe that you can actually practice technical skills while playing points. Conversely, the mental skills—communication and mental tough-ness—can only be honed and improved under the pressures of match play.

This chapter contains some suggestions for drills to improve the skills enumerated in this book. I have used all of them successfully in my teaching. The drills are grouped to-gether under the chapter headings for which they are most appropriate. Most of the drills are interchangeable, however, and can be used to sharpen more than just one skill.

SKILLS: EMOTIONAL AND TECHNICAL, BALANCE (CHAPTER ONE), COMMUNICATION (CHAPTER TWO), AND MENTAL TOUGHNESS (CHAPTER NINE)

The only way to practice the mental side of tennis—the teamwork, the communication skills and the toughness under pressure—is to make the commitment to play in practice exactly the way you want to play in a very important match. It is difficult to resist the temptation to play "hit and giggle" tennis when you are playing "just for fun," but the art of winning takes practice.

When playing practice matches, try to create some tension in the situation. Arrange to play people who are better than you are whenever possible. Play for lunch or a beer, and sign up for court number one instead of court number eighteen. Practice situational responses. If it is break-point and you are receiving serve, hit the very same shot you want to hit in the finals of the nationals. If you are serving at 30-40, hit the serve you need to capture a number one ranking. Take the same amount of time between points as you would if the match really mattered, and communicate with one another about a plan of attack as if your whole season hinged on winning this match. The ability to perform intelligently and calmly under pressure will not be there when you need it if you have to invent it on the spur of the moment. Like your forehand, it must be practiced. Play seriously in practice, play "up" when you can, and try never to lose.

To help you gain this confidence under pressure, use a crosscourt drill with your partner in which you, as server, get only one serve, which *must* go in, and in which you *cannot* miss your first volley. Your partner, the receiver, *must* get the service return in play and *must* make his first volley, after which the point is over. Under pressure, most points are lost on the third ball, and if each of you can be confident that you can always properly execute two balls, you will begin to play those important points with great assurance.

Another drill that will help you to develop better concentration and avoid making costly mental mistakes is the Everything Is Good Drill. Four players actually play points and keep score, but *every* ball on the court is deemed "good," whether it in fact bounces out or not. Play only stops when a ball hits the net or bounces twice. Players will find themselves playing "long" serves and chasing lobs that are really out, but it is a great drill for increasing hustle, avoiding the "oh, I thought it was going to be out" crucial error, and for overall levels of concentration throughout an entire point.

SKILL: PROPER COURT POSITION (CHAPTER THREE)

The best drill for court position is what I call the Take the Net Away Drill, along with its more sophisticated variations. To begin, one team holds second volley position while the team across the net is positioned defensively—that is, behind the base line. The net team must maintain its "wall" while being peppered with drives from the base line team which is intent upon drilling balls either between the two at the net or passing them in their alleys. If any ball falls unplayed between the net players, or if either player is passed in his alley, the team relinquishes the net to the opposition and must retreat to the base line. Meanwhile, the base line team practices good defense and approaches the net together if it receives the proper short ball. If all four players find themselves at the net in a rally, the team that wins the point on a placement volley keeps the net. No serving is allowed. Each rally is begun with a drop feed, and only one ball per rally is used. Remember the concept of "timing space" (chapters six and ten) and if your wall looks like Swiss cheese and you keep losing the net, a gut check on the quality of your volleys is in order.

When you have mastered this drill and it becomes boring, allow the base line team to try to drive the volleying team off the net by lobbing as well as by hitting passing shots. In this variation, the net team not only must defend against the passing shots, but also cannot allow a ball to *bounce behind them*, providing good overhead practice. If, however, a lob gets over their heads and bounces, they relinquish the net to their opponents. This drill works both sides of the net quite realistically since a base line team that has successfully put a ball over the heads of a net team would immediately take that opportunity to reclaim the net in actual match play.

One of the most difficult aspects of playing proper defense for a base line team is recognizing when a ball has landed in their court sufficiently "short" for them to reclaim the net. Sometimes, when I supervise this drill, I will ask a player to point to the spot in his court where a ball has bounced only to find his assessment off by as much as four or five feet. To attack this problem, I came up with a version of Take the Net Away that addresses the issue a little more directly.

All four players begin the point from a defensive court position, behind the base line. The rally is started with a drop feed (one ball in play amongst the four) and each team is responsible for recognizing when a ball bounces short enough on their side of the court to claim the net. They are responsible for communicating this fact to one another by saying "short," or "let's go," and for gaining second volley position *together*, as a team, without one player lagging woefully behind the other. Once a team has advanced to the net, the drill becomes exactly that described above and uses the same rules. While it is unrealistic to imagine a doubles point ever beginning with both teams playing defense, the value of the drill is in its insistence that players learn to recognize a short ball and react to it properly.

SKILL: INTELLIGENT SHOT SELECTION (CHAPTER FOUR)

Is my court position "deep" or "short"? Which of my opponents is closer to the net? Is this the time for an angle volley? Is this ball too low to hit down? Probably one-fourth of a second is not enough time to run through this litany and therefore you must replicate in your drills myriads of different situations and practice your responses to the given stimuli until they are absolutely automatic. (See diagrams 34 and 35.)

To avoid first volley indecision, serve fifty balls to the deuce court and fifty balls to the ad court, all the while chanting to yourself "inside ball down the middle, outside ball crosscourt" until you no longer have to think about it.

The best way to integrate the Deep to Deep, Short to Short Axiom into your tennis game is to isolate particular situations that occur repeatedly in match play and practice making the proper decision to the point of absolute satiety.

The server's partner faces the first critical decision concerning the deep or short options, and this drill helps him practice those choices:

Three players are needed for this drill, but a fourth makes it more interesting. A server serves a ball to the deuce court, after which his job is finished. A receiver hits the service return directly *at* the server's partner, after which *his* job is finished. It is incumbent upon the server's partner to determine whether the ball speeding toward him is high enough to change its direction, and thus should be played to the target in the receiver's partner's alley, or whether it is too low, and should be played back toward the receiver, "short to deep" to keep his team out of trouble. If a fourth player is involved, he should assume the hot seat position of receiver's partner in order to practice digging out balls aimed in his direction. The rally is not played out beyond this point in order that the server's partner may focus entirely on how he handles just one task. Be sure to give each player enough repetitions before rotating court positions. Changing places too

soon can disrupt a learner's rhythm just as he may be about to master the technique.

Another place critical judgment errors are made is on the overhead. Players either do not realize that they are too deep in the court to put the ball away and the opposition volleys it off for a winner, or they incorrectly play a shot which should be put away conveniently back to the waiting lobber. Try a drill which is a variation of the previous one. (See diagram 36.) All four players are positioned as above, but instead of driving the ball at the net player, the receiver lobs every service return over the server's partner, whose job it is to determine if he can put the ball away by aiming "short to short" into the receiver's partner's alley, or if, on impact, his court position will be so deep that he must play the ball back to the receiver, "deep to deep." Overheads are a personal matter, and each player will have to determine for himself where the boundary line between short and deep lies according to the limits of his own expertise.

Judgment errors are likely to be made when all four players are in a rapid-fire volley exchange because everyone is in a "short" court position and players either forget that they should not change the direction of a low ball, or they neglect to use a sharply angled volley as soon as they receive a ball with sufficient net clearance to allow them to hit down.

To sharpen your ability to recognize different heights of balls and make the proper

Diagram 34
Intelligent Shot Selection, Short or Deep Drill

In this drill, the server's partner is the worker. He knows that all balls will be hit at him. His task is to determine quickly the height of the ball aimed at him. His entire focus should be, "Can I hit down?" If no, the ball should be played "short to deep" to keep his team out of trouble. (See diagram 10.) If yes, the ball should be played "short to short" to end the point. (See diagram 10.) The entire exercise is designed to make the server's partner's judgment on ball height keener and thus his shot selection appropriate to the situation.

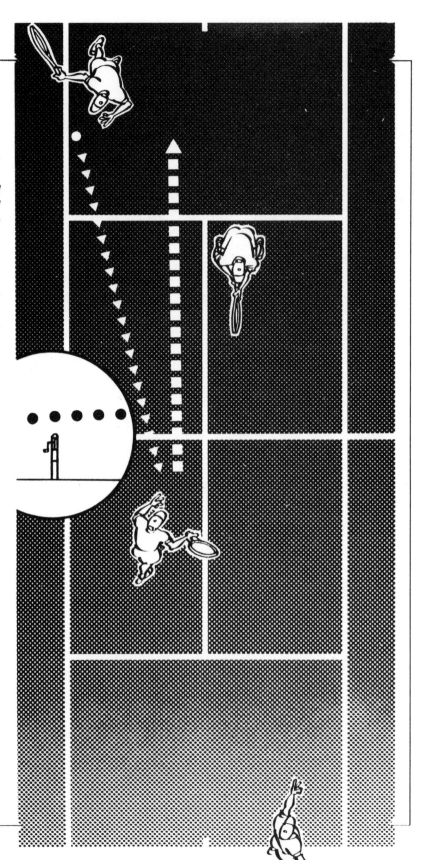

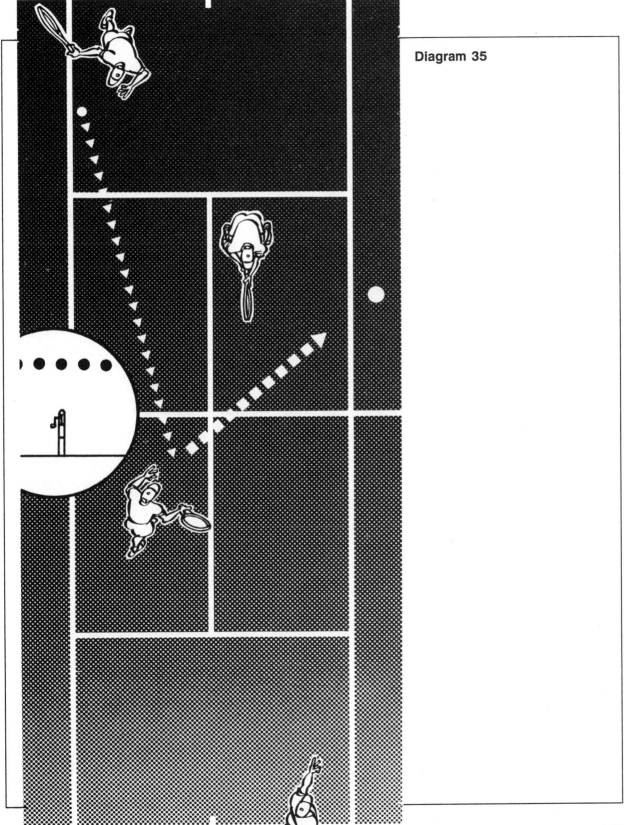

Diagram 35

Diagram 36
Intelligent Shot Selection, Overhead Drill

The server's partner knows that every ball off the receiver's racquet will be a lob over his head. He must experiment with his overhead and find for himself the depth of the lob that he can successfully terminate "short to short," and the limit of his expertise, after which he cannot punish the ball and it is deemed to be a "deep to deep" situation. The ability to make the overhead a putaway can be expanded with time and practice.

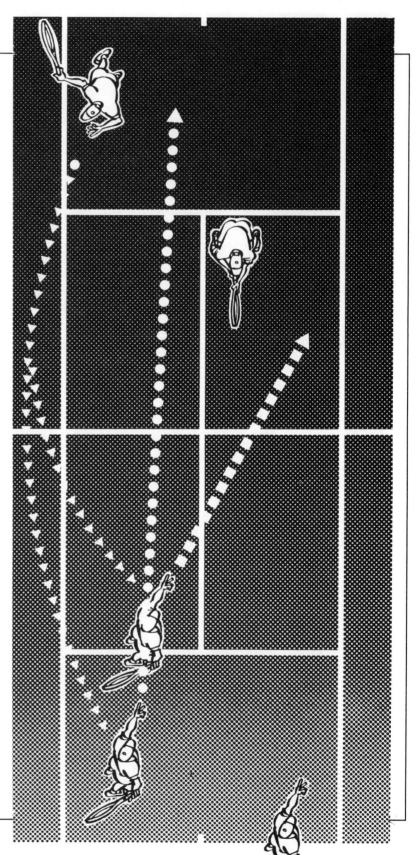

target selection, start with four players holding second volley position. The task is to keep one ball in play with each player aiming his shot directly down the middle and keeping it as low as possible. Soft volleys or half-volleys are desirable in order to give each player the maximum time to react. The first player to receive a ball with enough net clearance to hit down should immediately angle his volley to whichever alley target is most accessible to him, for which he receives five points. The angled putaway ends the point and a new rally is started. No points are awarded unless the ball actually lands in an alley because the drill is designed to teach players not to change the direction of low balls but to immediately change the direction of high balls.

Often players lose easy points because they fail to hit the primary target on the court—the ground—and end up hitting a racquet. A drill that my students really like is both fun and highly educational. Four players play points and keep score. All points are begun with a serve and played to conclusion, but the point is lost by any player whose ball hits an opponent's racquet before it hits the court. The rule is quite simple but players are immediately aghast at the number of points they lose and make adjustments very quickly.

SKILL: SUPERIOR POACHING SKILLS (CHAPTER FIVE)

Superior poaching skills are really superior volleying skills laced with a great deal of guts and courage. The first task of a coach trying to teach players to poach successfully is to convince them that yes, they really can get to that ball *way over there*. The second is to be honest with them about the number of humiliating mistakes they are going to make. The third is to keep each aspiring poacher's partner from huffily announcing, "You screwed up my shot."

If you are a player trying to become a superior poacher, it is difficult to believe that crossing into your partner's court and missing the volley is a better and more constructive idea than staying home and letting your partner play the ball. Ultimately, these sojourns across the net will pay dividends and contribute greatly to the health and sophistication of your doubles team.

In order to build confidence, start slowly. Practice a drill in which two players rally crosscourt from the base line while each of their partners begins in second volley position and tries to move across the net to intercept the ball. The poacher should take care to use the correct target—the alley toward which he is moving—and avoid the temptation to hit behind himself.

After you and your partner feel comfortable with this drill, try making things a little more realistic while still relying on a structured format. Orchestrate a drill amongst four players in which the rules are:

1. All serves are hit down the middle.
2. All service returns are hit back up the middle.

3. The server's partner *must* try to intercept the service return. He will hit high balls and defer to his partner on low balls, retreating and letting them go through.

4. If the server's partner misses the shot, the point is replayed.

This exercise helps both the poacher practice his technique and the server practice crossing behind his partner when appropriate. Be sure to give each player ample replications before rotating court positions.

When a team can execute both of these drills confidently, it is then time for them to experiment with using signals and to decide whether they ultimately wish to become a signaling team or a freelancing team.

SKILL: NET CONTROL (CHAPTER SIX)

The key words here are *team commitment*. If one partner is content to make his teammate the "gofer" while he idly looks on, preventative strategies will not be effective against the "lob queens."

The Take the Net Away Drill described earlier is an excellent way to practice not letting balls bounce behind you, and a variation of the drill is even better. Simply change the rules so that the base line team must lob *every* ball. Ground strokes are not permitted. While this removes the necessity for the net team to "read" whether a lob is in the offing, it does give them overhead practice on balls of varying heights and depths and makes them take balls in the air that they might otherwise allow to bounce.

For practice in keeping the service return lob covered properly, my students' favorite is the Scripted Return Drill.

Each player is handed a piece of paper which contains a list of service returns I have devised to be used when he is a receiver. The list is kept confidential by each player and might look something like this:

1. Crosscourt
2. Lob over net player
3. Lob down the center
4. Lob over net player
5. Crosscourt
6. Lob down the center

The serving team is aware that the returns of serve are preplanned and that each script contains a great number of lobs. It is the serving team's job to have a plan for covering the lob on each point and no lob is allowed to bounce. In this way, teams learn to anticipate the possibility of a lob and plan in advance how to cover it without relinquishing the net or having the server remain on the base line. This drill also encourages both partners to stay in constant communication with each other. Only the service return is scripted, and all points are played to conclusion. The receiver may inform his partner of his next scripted return.

SKILL: JOBS ON THE COURT (CHAPTER SEVEN)

The best doubles drill for all jobs on the court, including the poaching responsibilities of both the server's partner and the receiver's partner is Shadow Doubles. It can be played with two, three or four participants, and it can be cooperative or not. It tests all skills needed to play good doubles with the exception of the overhead, and even that could be added in a more creative version. (See diagram 37.)

In Shadow Doubles for two players, all balls must be played crosscourt, and the player who misfires in this respect loses the point. One player serves to his partner, who makes a crosscourt return. Each player must complete a successful first volley after which he moves to the second volley position. If the drill is cooperative, both players should hold an extra ball to be fed across the net immediately if an error is made. In this way, all points should contain a minimum of six or seven crosscourt volleys before the players are out of ammunition. Both players should make every effort to keep their volleys low and sufficiently crosscourt to avoid the poach of an imaginary partner. If the drill is to be noncooperative, then each player looks for the opportunity, *after* the first volley, to close the net and put the ball away. The putaway, too, must be played crosscourt.

If three players are to be involved, the server and receiver play the noncooperative version of the game, and the third player positions himself either as the server's partner or the receiver's partner, depending on which of those poaching skills needs the most work. Regardless of which job he assumes,

his task is to try to enter the point and put the ball away in the direction of the proper target; thus he is exempt from the crosscourt rule.

If four players participate, each player should keep his job, that is, server, server's partner, receiver or receiver's partner, for at least ten points. In this way, the receiving team can practice executing their responsibilities repeatedly, without having to change "hats" on each point. No lobs are permitted and the point is played to its conclusion.

The basic structure of Shadow Doubles is the keystone for improving your expertise in every job you must execute on the court. It is well worth improvising versions for areas of weakness not covered above. Practice for long periods of time, but always quit before you get bored, tired or sloppy.

SKILL: FLEXIBILITY (CHAPTER EIGHT)

Again, it cannot be overemphasized that you must practice the way you intend to play, and it is not enough to practice that way for just a few points. If your team is a bit shaky on how to use the Australian formation, play an entire match using it on every service point. If having to start a point from behind the base line gives you an anxiety attack, play an entire match starting every point from that position. You do not need to use unusual formations in every match you play, but when the moment of necessity arrives, your flexibility must be smooth, confident and practiced, not the last resort of a team unprepared

Diagram 37
Jobs on the Court, Shadow Doubles Drill

Shadow Doubles, so named because each player has a phantom partner, is the most important doubles drill a team can practice. So long as the ball is kept crosscourt, players can use it to hone point-ending skills; to be cooperative with one another and count the number of balls played across the net; to practice closing the net and executing sharply angled volleys; or to simply practice serving and gaining their net position from the base line. The possibilities are endless. All good doubles partners practice some form of this drill at least two-to-three hours per week. Servers and receivers always start the point. You could not do better than to practice starting it to your advantage—endlessly.

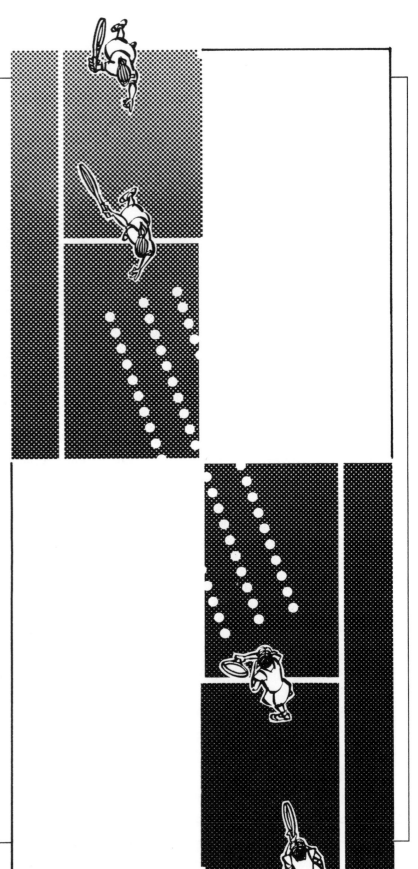

for adversity. Don't forget to ask your friendly adversaries to use all of the unusual formations against you, too, and often. There is no excuse for you, as a receiver, to panic if the opposition lines up against you in the Australian formation. Practice against it until you are as comfortable as you are hitting crosscourts.

One drill that my students really appreciate is the Ping-Pong Drill. It has no real value as far as actual doubles skills are concerned, but it helps communication, breaks up rigid thinking about "your side of the court" and "my side of the court," encourages players to be flexible, and it is fun.

All four players begin on the base line. One ball is kept in play by all four, and each point is started with a drop feed. There is only one rule in the drill: No one player on either side of the net can hit two balls in a row. This means that when a player strikes a ball, his partner is responsible for the next, no matter where in the court it bounces. Players may choose to take the net or not, to use an "i" formation, or an automatic "switch" in court positions. Points are played to conclusion but immediately lost if a player on a team hits two balls in a row. Score is kept like Ping-Pong, with the winning team needing twenty-one points. An added benefit to the drill is that it aids racquet-watching skills since each player *knows* exactly which ball is his to play, no matter how far he must travel to reach it.

SKILL: COMMAND OF THE INTANGIBLES (CHAPTER TEN)

There is no drill that will allow you to practice taking more time to hit a ball other than your determination to increase it. Similarly, there is no magic formula drill that will endow your doubles game with the perfect selection of depth, pace or touch on every ball except the number of court hours you devote to the endeavor. There are, however, several drills that I have designed to improve students' racquet-watching skills, their movement, anticipation and hand-eye coordination. (See diagram 38.)

The best and simplest way to check on or improve your racquet-watching skills is to position yourself astride the center service line in second volley position. Ask your partner to stand behind the base line opposite you and feed you a ball, after which he is to move radically either to the left or right. You should be able to see this movement and volley competently into the open court. If you are initially unsuccessful, keep trying. Eye control does not take long to improve with a little diligence.

For better and more balanced movement forward, position yourself on the base line crosscourt from your partner, who should be in second volley position. Begin the rally with a drop feed and move forward after each ball you hit, taking care to make a split-stop every time your partner hits the ball. His task is to aim every one of his volleys at your feet, moving closer and closer on each ball. Thus

Diagram 38
Command of the Intangibles Drill

The net player is positioned in the center of the court—not a position normally assumed in doubles. He assumes his position in order to practice moving radically left or right. The practice partner on the opposite base line feeds a ball and quickly moves left or right. This movement will occur before his ball actually crosses the net. In the time it takes for the ball to cross the net, the volleyer should be able to read not only the direction of the ball, but also the lateral movement of the player who has struck the ball if his eyes are glued to his opponent. This exercise teaches a player to watch an opponent's racquet, footwork and body repositioning at the same time that he must watch a ball coming toward him. Four eyes would be better, but we only have two. Great doubles players make two do the work of four.

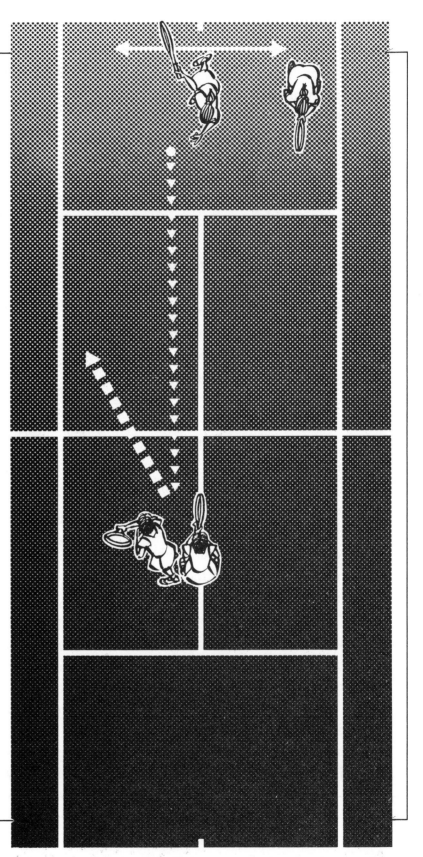

he must shorten his aim point farther forward on each of his volleys as you approach the net. He is not to hit away from you but rather he is to try to hit your shoes. You, as the approacher, will find yourself having to hit difficult volleys or half-volleys on your journey toward the net. You win the point if you can attain your second volley position diagonally opposite your partner. Drills are only effective if they are more difficult than match play, and although an unrealistic expectation, if you can begin from the base line against a player already entrenched at the net and claim your own volley position, you most certainly will improve your volleying skills, your forward movement and your balance.

Anticipation is a skill acquired over time, but to practice learning what happens when you take away an opponent's timing space, or what happens when you don't, try a simple crosscourt drill. Position yourself at the net in second volley position and have your partner begin crosscourt from you on the base line. Ask him to hit any kind of shot he wishes, so long as he keeps it crosscourt. Within the rally, experiment with different depth volleys and note the height of your partner's response to each of your volleys as it clears the net. In this way, you will begin to learn what is possible and impossible for a player in trouble or a player in no difficulty whatsoever. Count how many times his ball is rising as it clears the net when you volley deep

enough to remove his timing space, and note what happens when you don't.

Two drills help develop quick hands around the net. The first gives two players quite a workout and the second may give one player quite a scare.

The Endless Volley Drill has no net. One player positions himself at the "T," but faces the fence. His partner stands about two feet from the fence facing his partner. Players are encouraged to hit rapid-fire volleys, and since there is no net, points are virtually endless. Students quickly find that they must bring their racquets to ready position at a lightning-like speed, that *every* ball comes back and that their ability to react to hard-hit balls improves dramatically. Again, making the drill more difficult than the match play engenders rapid improvement.

The Serve at Your Partner Drill is not for the fainthearted, but it is effective. A player positions himself in second volley position in either the deuce or ad court while his partner serves first serves at him. The benefits for developing quicker hands at the net are obvious, but the drill can backfire if a player's volleying skills are not up to the drill. Some players may need to work into it slowly, starting back farther than second volley position and asking their partners to begin by lobbing serves at them.

IN CONCLUSION

The proof of your practice, of course, manifests itself in your match play record. I have included a charting sheet that I use to check my students' progress (see page 129). New computer technology can duplicate much of the information, but not all of it. Computers cannot tell if the proximate cause of the point being lost was a judgment error or a positioning mistake, or even if the point was lost due to poor shot selection. Although these judgments are subjective, I feel they are better indicators of a team's overall progress toward mastery than the dry statistics produced by a machine.

Ultimately, there is no such thing as a useless drill, and no substitute for court hours. Use your imagination and devise drills that isolate the parts of your doubles game that make you feel insecure. And remember that it is a silly quirk of fate that the more you practice the luckier you become.

Date:		
	Player:	Player:
First Serve	As a matter of interest, check here if missed.	
Double Fault		
FHSR		
BHSR		
First Volley		
Second Volley		
Lob		
Overhead		
Poach		
Bad Judgment		
Poor Position		
Bad Shot Selection		
Good Placement	Check here if a point was won on a good placement.	
Winner	Check here if service ace, service return winner, etc.	
Opponent Forced Error	Check here if your player simply could not return opponent's great shot.	

A check mark goes on whichever of these lines actually caused the point to be lost.

GENERAL OBSERVATIONS:

- Did the team play with confidence?
- Were they too predictable?
- Did they visibly lose heart?
- Did they respond positively to the challenge of pressure?
- Were they flexible enough to use different formations when they needed them?

INDEX

Get the Most Out of Life With
Betterway Books

Roughing It Easy—Have fun in the great outdoors with these ingenious tips! You'll learn what equipment to take, how to plan, set up a campsite, build a fire, backpack—even how to camp during winter with this astounding guidebook of camping and cooking hints. *ISBN 0-9621257-3-3, paperback, 256 pages, #70260-K*

Recipes for Roughing It Easy—Don't let leaving the kitchen behind stop you from making meals the whole family will love! This book collects the top one hundred recipes for campers, hikers and lovers of the outdoors. Dian Thomas, author of the legendary book *Roughing It Easy*, shows you how to pack, prepare and cook fun, flavorful meals anywhere, anytime, for every occasion. *ISBN 0-9621257-8-4, paperback, 192 pages, #70530-K*

Backyard Roughing It Easy—Make the most of your family's quality time just steps from your own back door. This wonderful reference is packed with ideas for outdoor fun, tasty recipes and simple ways to turn household items into usable outdoor gear. *ISBN 0-9621257-5-X, paperback, 192 pages, #70366-K*

Holiday Fun Year-Round with Dian Thomas—A year-round collection of festive crafts and recipes to make virtually every holiday a special and memorable event. You'll find exciting ideas that turn mere holiday observances into opportunities to exercise imagination and turn the festivity all the way up—from creative Christmas gift-giving to a super Super Bowl party. *ISBN 0-9621257-2-5, paperback, 144 pages, #70300-K*

Clutter's Last Stand—Don Aslett, America's #1 cleaning expert, shows you how to get rid of clutter once and for all, in every area of your life. This proven, practical guide is packed with humorous anecdotes, cartoons, quizzes and insightful advice that makes streamlining your life a snap! *ISBN 0-89879-137-5, paperback, 280 pages, #01122-K*

For Packrats Only—Learn how to clean up, clear out, and de-junk your life forever! This companion to the best-selling Clutter's Last Stand details a step-by-step "de-clutter" program, complete with charts, checklists and informative sidebars that help you get control of your living and storage spaces. *ISBN 0-937750-25-5, paperback, 232 pages, #70565-K*

How to Have a 48-Hour Day—Get more done and have more fun as you double what you can do in a day! Aslett reveals reasons to be more productive everywhere—and what "production" actually is. You'll learn how to keep accomplishing despite setbacks, ways to boost effectiveness, the things that help your productivity and much more. *ISBN 0-937750-13-1, paperback, 160 pages, #70339-K*

Don Aslett's Clutter-Free! Finally and Forever—Free yourself of unnecessary stuff that chokes your home and clogs your life! If you feel owned by your belongings, you'll discover incredible excuses people use for allowing clutter, how to beat the "no-time" excuse, how to determine what's junk, how to prevent recluttering and much more! *ISBN 0-937750-12-3, paperback, 224 pages, #70306-K*

Make Your House Do the Housework, Revised Edition—Take advantage of new work-saving products, materials and approaches, to make your house keep itself in order. You'll discover page after page of practical, environmentally-friendly new ideas and methods for minimizing home cleaning and maintenance. This book includes charts that rate materials and equipment. Plus, you'll find suggestions for approaching everything from simple do-it-yourself projects to remodeling jobs of all sizes. *ISBN 1-55870-384-5, paperback, 208 pages, #70293-K*

The Insider's Guide to Buying a New or Used Car, 3rd Edition—Learn how to give yourself the upper hand in negotiations, get the best deals on trade-ins, new car prices, special options and financing. Burke Leon provides guidelines for recognizing and countering manipulative dealer tactics, evaluating the value of a used car, buying a car on the Web and more! *ISBN 1-55870-566-X, paperback, 256 pages, #70494-K*

*These books and other fine Betterway titles
are available from your local bookstore, online supplier or by calling*
1-800-448-0915.